WHAT PEOPLE ARE SAYING

No! Maybe? Yes! is a page turner from the start as well as inspirational, empowering, and unique. Written by Grace Stevens who changed her life at age 64 by allowing herself to live her dreams. The change was complicated, but as Grace reveals, nothing is impossible. *No! Maybe? Yes!* allows the reader to join in Grace's journey while possibly discovering one's own centered, connected, and passionate life. A book I have been waiting for to put on my office shelf.

—Peg Hurley Dawson
  Licensed Mental Health Counselor, Certified Sex Therapist

As a parent of a young transman, Grace's book has not only helped provide insight as to what his journey may have been like, but has also inspired me to reflect on my own journeys—past, present, and future—to live my own truth.

—Carol Caravana, Teacher and Parent

You have truly nailed our journeys to share, to educate others, and to begin creating an understanding of just who we really are, a none-too-easy task to take on.

—Jenny Robinson, Gender Justice League

In *No! Maybe? Yes!* Grace Stevens takes her audience along on her midlife journey from "he" to "she," or more accurately, from "they" to "we" as she describes in heart-opening detail her internal tug of war over gender expression and representation. Allowing the reader an intimate view of her internal struggle, she poignantly depicts each part of her—those that vowed to protect, those that tenaciously resisted change, those that tugged forward in silent revolution, and those that tempered the pace to keep the peace.

Grace shows us how to give expression to the deepest, most vital needs, fears, desires, and gifts within, through discovering, reclaiming, and honoring what each part represents and then giving each a hand in the creation of her own inner masterpiece, reflected by her gradual, dramatic external transformation. Most importantly, Grace offers an example of how to make friends with fear, to humbly accept uncertainty, to negotiate with vying parts for meeting the conflicting needs, and to live out her desires, giving birth to her most precious gifts. She engages our curiosity, steals our heart, brings us on an adventure, and in the final chapters, teaches us a more expansive way of understanding the concepts of gender, sex, and sexuality on a continuum versus binary basis, and as fluid rather than solid in nature. Opening to all possibilities and variances, Grace evolves herself and her audience to fascinating new paradigms for the expression of humanness and humanity. Bravo, Grace! Bravo!

—Anita L. Masterson, LICSW, Program Coordinator/Social Worker, Alternative Education Program Wachusett Regional High School

No! Maybe? Yes!

Living My Truth

No! Maybe? Yes!

Living My Truth

Grace Anne Stevens

Graceful Change Press . Lexington

No! Maybe? Yes! Living My Truth

© 2015 Grace Anne Stevens
Graceful Change Press
ISBN 978-0-9863003-0-1

Contact:
Grace Stevens
(781) 789-6103
gas333@verizon.net
www.graceannestevens.com

314 Bedford Street
Apt 105
Lexington MA 02420

Printed in the United States of America

DEDICATION

To Tessa, my BFF, who was the first person I shared my shameful secret with. Her first response was, "Whatever floats your boat." I thank you for sharing the past decade with me and teaching me so much.

Tessa pointed out that almost every time she asked me to do something, my response started with a harsh *No!* Although disappointed, she often continued to ask again, and I slowly moved to *Maybe?* and then eventually a *Yes!* Although I was happy and excited to get to this position of Yes! I had some trouble understanding her frustration with my process.

It took some time to realize I was living my entire life with this as my primary instruction set. I am only now beginning to realize how difficult this has been for all those I have been in a relationship with.

We said our goodbyes when I transitioned, but they did not stick, as we both learned that the meaning of true friendship was more important than my changing gender.

Everyone has his own specific vocation or mission in life; everyone must carry out a concrete assignment that demands fulfillment. Therein, he cannot be replaced nor can his life be repeated. Thus, everyone's task is unique as is his specific opportunity to implement it.

—Viktor E. Frankl, *Man's Search for Meaning*

CONTENTS

FOREWORD

This book is fascinating at a number of levels. First, it is an impressive memoir, well written with candor and vulnerability that documents the struggle of someone to first recognize and then begin to live their truth. A unique aspect of this memoir that is of particular interest to me as a career-long student of internal systems, is that Grace lets us in, not only on how her relationships with family, friends, and colleagues evolved, but she also provides a rare window into the inner world of parts or sub-personalities and how those inner relationships change simultaneous to the outer ones. She has amazing recall of both inner and outer detail that brings her process to life such that you identify with her journey whether or not your issues revolve around gender.

Second, Grace's memoir not only provides transgender people with a potential map for their journeys, so they can anticipate the boulders in the road and have examples for how to navigate them, it also can inspire anyone who dares to listen inside and realizes that they are not living their truth, whether that involves the wrong career, relationship, life style, or gender. Most of us have parts that won't let us really listen because the consequences of making those changes seem so daunting and the way things are don't seem that bad. This was certainly true for Grace who had created a conventional life as a man and faced huge life disruption and potential humiliation as she began attending to her female inner voice.

We are a collectivist species. As human beings there is little scarier than being shunned by the herd. In changing her gender, Grace risked losing connection to all the people that she relied on and who relied on her. Most of us are not willing to take such a risk without a model of how it can lead to vast improvements in inner and outer peace. The inclusion of Grace's inner dialogues provides an example of how we can help those fearful parts of us trust our leadership and not feel so dependent on the herd. The ultimate positive outcome in both her relationships with her children and friends as well as the new harmony among her parts shows us that these risks can be worth it.

Third, as an explorer of inner systems, I am intrigued by several questions that kept emerging throughout the book. The big one is what is the relationship among gender identity, parts, and Self? Relatedly, does what I call Self, which could be analogous to soul or spirit or essence, have a gender? In addition, what is the driving force in Grace's inner system that made her ultimately conclude that the female voice was speaking the truth about her identity? Is gender identity a trait that organizes inner systems and can't be affected by them, like height or race, and unlike those traits, is sometimes independent of genetics? How can we tell when the inner voice that says we are not in the right body is our truth and is not the product of some kind of trauma that left us hating our body or our genitalia?

I don't pretend to know all the answers to those questions, but Grace's journey may provide some hints. For Grace, there was always a kind of knowing that she was female, a knowledge that the rest of her system organized to try to deny. The representative of this knowing was the female part of her who fought fiercely to break through the denial and manifest this identity as fully as possible. As this part increasingly prevailed, the other male parts slowly came around, overcoming their socialization and fear to recognize and ultimately celebrate the correctness of her position.

I have always known that I was male and, despite having found some female parts of me, I can imagine that if I had been born into a female body, from an early age I would have a strong abiding sense that something was wrong. Perhaps a male part of me would become the crusader for my masculine identity and would fight his way into ascendency in my inner system in the way Grace's female part did in hers. I can only hope that I would have the courage to listen to him and not live my life in turmoil and secrecy.

Yet I have worked with sex abuse survivors who hated their bodies and wished to be the opposite gender. These were mainly women who, when we worked with their parts, revealed that their motives were protective—parts thought that being a man would mean not being attacked or would mean having more power. I think it would have been a mistake for those clients to have become transgender, and in fact, after we were able to heal those parts they became much more content with the bodies they were in.

So it's complicated, and like so many volatile issues, it is easy for groups to universalize and say that gender identity is merely a social construct or that the desire to be in a different body is the product trauma or pathology, or on the other side, that it is always due to a predetermined, hardwired, nature.

My solution to this conundrum is to help people listen carefully to their parts, heal what needs to be healed, and then see where they land on whatever issue they face when the smoke clears a bit. If someone comes to me wanting to divorce, for example, I will ask that they give me some sessions to explore the motives of the parts that are lobbying for it before they make the final decision. Often, after a series of explorations, it becomes clear to the client that it was a group of burdened parts that took over to get away from pain that can be healed other ways, and they stay in the marriage or the opposite: the client becomes increasingly convinced of the authenticity of the original decision and can proceed with their Self in the lead and their parts in harmony around it.

This is what Grace did, with the help of the IFS model, and that process is reflected in her parts' dialogues. The more she listened the clearer she became that the female part's insistence was not the result of pathology and instead was the expression of something fundamental about her. My experience is when a part is expressing a fundamental truth, that becomes evident fairly quickly, and we then work with the parts that fear the consequences of living that truth.

Richard Schwartz, Ph.D.
Developer of the Internal Family Systems Model
Adjunct Faculty, Department of Psychiatry,
Harvard Medical School

PREFACE

Snowflakes

I'm looking out my window, and snowflakes are falling. They slowly drift out of the sky and give me an impression they have no direction, destination, or urgency to get anywhere.

I am not looking very closely at any single snowflake as it dawns on me that I know, or at least I have been taught, that no two snowflakes are the same. I have always accepted this as the truth; I have seen a few pictures of different snowflakes, yet I have never taken the time or trouble to actually look at snowflakes to verify it. Have you?

I am like a snowflake! So are you! You, and I, and each of the more than seven billion people that share this planet are unique. Most of us either take this for granted or forget it. In our very human need to belong, to be taken care of, our brains are wired to sort through those who are like us and those who are different. We often unconsciously sort and categorize, and then our culture will add labels of good and bad to these groupings.

If there are groups we do not know about, our large but finite brains try to simplify, group, and categorize them. Sometimes, when we see something that does not fit into a known pattern, it is simpler for us to reject and label it bad than it is to learn about it, sort it, and add it to our personal database of knowledge. Getting educated requires work! Sometimes we are not willing to do this work, sometimes we are.

I am a member of one of these smaller groups. I am transgender.

It seems to me that when someone crosses, rejects, or straddles the gender divide, most people would like to have simple answers so they can categorize what may not meet their binary maps of gender, sex, anatomy, and biology. They might say they want to understand, but I suspect that is the word they use when they want to see where to store it in their brain. Actual understanding of the experience, which will be unique for each transgender person, may be difficult, so simplifying by categorizing suffices for many. Meanwhile, some people will be unwilling to learn or accept what is new and different, which can result in rejection, judgment, bullying, and labeling. It escapes me how this can be the easier path for these people.

However, the fact remains: all people are like snowflakes. Transgender people are like snowflakes—no two are the same. This is true of their stories, their feelings, their desires, their needs. It is true for my story and equally true for your story. Each person's story and life are unique! When we are willing to be open and learn about our differences, our uniqueness, and accept each other, aren't we all better for it?

My Hopes

My personal journey to living my truth was about accepting that I was transgender and at long last, making the decision to do something about it. My intention for this narrative is to extend my message of "Living My Truth" to invite and encourage you to "Live Your Truth." This is for everyone without exception! It is a universal message and cry.

- Are you living *your* life or are there fears and concerns, judgments and doubts that hold you back?

- Do you give up your inner and true self in order to please others or what you think might please them?

- Do you suffer in isolation with shame and longing?

I know these feelings, and can say it feels better each day as I am living my truth! I was prepared for losses, and was lucky enough to not have suffered them. I know not all who live their truth are so lucky.

People say I inspire them. People say I have courage. I never think of these as characteristics that describe me. I only know that I am free from the internal voices that told me I was lying and not living the life of who I truly am. The voices stopped and allowed me to be free to live each moment. I don't have the answers to all of life's puzzles, and this is fine. I can now ask questions that I was afraid to ask before and be willing to seek an answer. This is enough for me.

Do you have your own unanswered questions? Perhaps living your truth may also be enough for you.

TRANSITION

tran·si·tion [tran-**zish**-*uh* n, -**sish**-]

noun

1. Movement, passage, or change from one position, state, stage, subject, concept, etc., to another; change: the transition from adolescence to adulthood.

2. *Music*

a. a passing from one key to another; modulation.
b. a brief modulation; modulation used in passing.
c. a sudden, unprepared modulation.

3. A passage from one scene to another by sound effects, music, etc., as in a television program, theatrical production, or the like.

verb (used without object)

4. To make a transition: He had difficulty transitioning from enlisted man to officer.

Origin: 1545–55; < Latin trānsitiōn- (stem of trānsitiō) a going across, equivalent to trānsit (us) (past participle of transīre to cross; cf. transit) + -iōn- -ion

Note: Excerpt from Dictionary.com.

THE PATH OF MOST RESISTANCE

What is needed, rather than running away or controlling or suppressing or any other resistance, is understanding fear; that means, watch it, learn about it, come directly into contact with it. We are to learn about fear, not how to escape from it.

—Jiddu Krishnamurti

Will You Still Need Me?

Will you still need me, will you still feed me, when I'm sixty-four?

—"When I'm Sixty Four,"
John Lennon and Paul McCartney

I was a few months shy of my sixty-fourth birthday when I transitioned my gender.

When most people my age are thinking about slowing down and retirement, I was planning on living a life that I never thought possible. A life where I would be true to who I really am.

I used to say that I was consciously aware of my gender issues since I was eight years old. As you will soon learn, I discovered these issues go even further back.

My life's story seemed pretty complete. I was married for twenty-five years and have three adult kids. I will always be their dad! I coached all my kids' sports for over a decade. I walked the dogs. I helped the kids deliver the newspapers on their routes. I got divorced. I worked for over forty years in the high-tech industry with twenty-five years in various engineering management roles.

I was already familiar with reinventing myself. It seems that once each decade I found myself unemployed and was lucky enough to find a new and mostly better job within the tech field. In 2004, I was lucky to find a technical position after being out of the industry for two years. (Damn dot-com implosion!) In 2005, I returned to school. I have received two degrees forty years apart, a bachelor's degree of engineering (1969) and a master's in counseling psychology (2009). From 2009 to 2013, I worked in dual careers, as a technical program manager during the day and as a mental health counselor in the evenings. My brain and my emotions were being exercised in vastly different arenas.

Yet, for so many years, there was not a night when I went to sleep or a morning when I woke up that I experienced anything other than the dissonance of being untrue to the gender identity I knew I was, while all outward signs belied that inner truth. My internal struggle had so many nuances with parts of me fighting battle after battle for being true, while others denied it. Many parts of me worried about the shame, the discovery, and the potential losses of being my true self. How could this old guy, who had a pretty good collection of Old Guys Rule T-shirts, live in the world as the woman who I truly was? *There was no way!*

"When I get older, losing my hair": I started to lose my hair around thirty years before transitioning...at least the hair on my head. Although not quite a Wookie, the rest of my body had short fur everywhere. *There was no way!*

"Will you still need me, will you still feed me?" Contrary to the optimism of "When I'm Sixty Four," this was my most difficult decision on the journey to living my truth. What if my family and kids abandoned me? Was the risk of being true worth the risk of abandonment? *There was no way!*

Living with a secret for decade upon decade was taking its toll on me. My relationship with myself was in effect nonexistent. I lived my life playing a role that I thought I should to survive. I protected my secret fiercely, not only from everyone else, but also from myself. All the outward trappings of success were losing any meaning, as if they ever had any. *There had to be a way!*

As my journey morphed from the decades of saying NO! of denial and impossibility to the questioning of MAYBE? to the decision of YES! I learned so much, not only about myself, but how common yet different each of our own journeys may be. I was surprised by how my journey has impacted others as well as the further reinventions I have experienced since taking it.

Surprise became amazement. Along this journey, I acquired a mission, part of which is to share my story with you.

Drawn and Quartered:
Befriending My Parts

A part of me kept screaming, "Be a Man!"

While another part could not stop laughing while thinking, "Who are you fooling?"

I had a part that got so turned on by girls; that wanted the sex, the pleasure, the release, the intimacy.

Another part took me to flights of fantasy and then scolded me for hiding my truth.

There were many more…arguing and fighting and judging and criticizing and making all sorts of noise.

These conflicting parts were tearing me apart from different directions. At the time, I had no idea that each had their own single mission—to protect and save me—to save me from something they each thought I could never handle. I tried to shut them all down in many various ways. This proved impossible.

I suspect that most people can relate to the "voices" in their head that may argue, criticize, judge, be afraid, act impulsively, or hold back any action at all. In the Internal Family Systems (IFS) Model, these are called "parts." The parts are thought of as distinct sub-personalities. As we grow up the parts can become trapped, learning their own beliefs and acquiring burdens. Sometimes a part of us will take over, or overwhelm our system, and we seem to be acting or saying things that do not really feel like us. Sometimes we are aware that this is happening, but many times we are not. The therapeutic goal of IFS therapy is to help us build a relationship with our parts so that they do not overwhelm us, and we can understand their fears and concerns. By providing what is called self-leadership, you let all the parts know that you are present and can bring safety to their entire system.

I learned about IFS in 2009 and began training in the model right after I graduated from Lesley University. When I graduated in May 2009 with a master's in counseling psychology, I thought that I was just another wounded healer added to the world. Whatever made me think that I could help people, when I could not even be true to myself?

Internal Family Systems training changed my life. During introductions I announced, "I am transgender and on a journey that I will share with all that are present." I thought that this would be safe—after all, this was a room filled with forty to fifty therapists!

After the first three days of training, I identified three of my parts: Fear, Shame, and Confusion. I learned that they believed their jobs were to protect me. I created a new relationship with each of them and found their concerns and assured them that everything would be OK if I pursued a journey to live my truth.

This was not easy work and took some time. I slowly learned to work with my parts and to help others work with theirs. Throughout my story, you will meet many of my parts, as they share what they were thinking and feeling, and see how I learned to become a leader so my parts no longer needed to overwhelm me. This is my story—my memoir, but it is really a story with many voices telling it.

I don't believe I could have taken this journey without the IFS model. For those who would like to learn more about this model, check out www.selfleadership.org.

Sex and Gender

It would be so much simpler if the concepts of gender and sex and sexual orientation were binary and aligned as so many people might think. Alas, it turns out to be not true.

Many people often will use the terms sex and gender interchangeably. Yes, it is simple and easy to create a single category for these concepts. The words *gender* and *sex* both convey in the same sense: state of being male or female. However, they are typically used in slightly different ways: sex tends to refer to biological differences, while gender refers to cultural or social ones.

The complexity of what we may think of as sex and gender can be broken into five separate and—here is the important fact—independent constructs. These entities are:

- **Sex:** biology, anatomy, chromosomes

- **Gender Identity:** psychological sense of self

- **Gender Expression:** communication of gender

- **Sexual Orientation:** identity of erotic response

- **Sexual Behaviors:** what and with whom sexual acts occur

It has taken a good part of the past fifty years for the majority of people to come to an understanding that one's sexual orientation is not chosen but innately wired in their brains. The fight for LGB rights has been ongoing as is the present fight for acceptance and allowance of same-sex marriages.

In recent years, there is the beginning of understanding the journeys of the transgender population. There is so much more work to do, and it will take time to educate everyone that gender identity is also innately prewired in our brains. For people like me, the challenge has been to understand what is happening to us, our internal feelings and self-knowledge while our culture has had few examples of acceptance, modeling, or understanding of this facet of human development. Are we good? Bad? Broken? Or are we OK to just be who we know we are?

I am one of those people who has known about my gender issues my entire life and kept it buried deep inside. Today we see children who clearly acknowledge or recognize that their gender identity does not match their biology as early as two years old, and with loving, supportive, and learning parents, they are able to live their truth early on. However, there are also those who are not allowed to be themselves or feel accepted, and will lead lives of suffering, confusion, and fear, and will unfortunately resort to forms of self-harm. We know this can end badly.

No, Maybe, Yes

How do you relate in the world?

- **Are you a people pleaser?** Do you say yes when you may really want to say no? You may deny your own needs, wants, and desires for a variety of reasons and give yourself up in the service of others.

- **Are you a non-committer?** Is your initial response a strong and often harsh NO? You may not have even processed the request fully but your negativity is broadcast quickly and widely. If you process and change your position, are you confused why people don't jump right on board with you?

- **Are you a non-decider?** You can't or won't make a decision. Do you second-guess yourself? Perhaps you have self-doubt or worry you will be criticized. What if someone were to tell you that you shouldn't feel what you feel? Your response to a choice is usually MAYBE. No matter what the results are, you may still not be satisfied and wonder what might have happened if you had chosen the other path.

No matter how you relate externally, you also have an internal relationship with all your parts. They all are protecting you, but the question is what are they protecting you from? For me, they were protecting me from living my truth.

Fear, shame, and confusion have happily taken on new jobs. The new jobs are communicator/teacher, with pride and clarity, and storyteller.

Author's Note: Music Hath Charms...♪

As you will soon learn, working with feelings has been a challenge for most of my life. However, I realized that music and songs allowed me and my parts to travel to places, and help me process feelings that I struggled with in most of my waking moments. I use songs, either titles or short lyrics, throughout this book to help convey and set a background to help you get a sense of my journey. I often have lacked the words to convey the experience in any other manner.

Welcome to my story.

No!

*I think the greatest illusion we have is that denial protects us.
It's actually the biggest distortion and lie. In fact, staying
asleep is what's killing us.*

—Eve Ensler

First Journey

She didn't know when she knew. But know, she did! Although this whole awareness and sensing thing was still so new to her, there was so much that she knew!

Changes were coming, and coming quickly. She was so used to the gentle rocking and the regular rhythm—Ba–Bmmm...Ba–Bmmm...Ba–Bmmm—that was always in the background. She was aware of her own rhythm from inside of her—b-ba..b-ba..b-ba—that although faster than the background, seemed to be matching it in some way. This was all so familiar. She could not remember not being present with all of this. This was home, the only home she knew, but now she realized, it was almost time to leave.

She loved the familiar, gentle rocking. She even enjoyed feeling herself gently bumping into what must have been a wall of some sort, and even when something pushed her back away from it. She always thought she heard some laughing from a place far away when this happened. Every now and again, she rocked herself and changed position. When she did, she knew that the laughter was her own.

The first time the wave hit her she was scared. The background noises were loud; the rhythms everywhere speeded up and buffeted her about in all directions. Her own rhythms speeded up, and she squeezed herself into an even tighter ball than she was already in. Then it subsided, and things returned to the way they were. But from somewhere deep inside, she knew that soon she would leave this place, this home. She wondered how long it would take.

Even though she noticed the next wave coming, she was still not prepared. It was louder, stronger, and longer than the first one. It, too, subsided, and she tried to go deeper inside to see if she knew what would be next. She did not have to wait too long before she could sense another wave building, and then there were more of those far away voices that she had heard before, although they were no longer laughing. There was yelling and then everything started moving. She was being rocked and bounced as the next wave came crashing down on her and again she squeezed herself tighter and tighter to withstand it.

She knew they were moving and that she was not the only one being uncomfortable, when she heard a loud popping sound and was thrown from side to side and she realized that bumping into the wall now was no longer fun. Another wave was starting up. They were coming closer together, and then she faded out....

She didn't know how long she was out, but as her awareness returned, she sensed she was being pushed around and
turned upside down. At first she wanted to fight it, but she
knew that it was time to take the journey. As the next wave was
building, she tried her best to relax and just ride it out. She knew
she was being squeezed through a tunnel...one that she seemed
to be making as her head was plowing its way through, being
pushed by wave after wave. She could feel her own rhythms
beating faster than ever...ba...ba...ba...ba...ba. She suddenly
felt something grabbing and pulling her out of the tunnel a little
bit at a time as each wave was pushing her forward.

She didn't know how, but she knew it was time to open
her eyes. It hurt and she cried. She thought that the worst was
over, and later she told me over and over how she wished that
were the case. At this point is when she felt all the problems began.

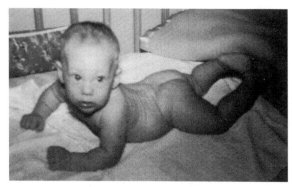

It's a boy, or is it?

There were
bright lights every-
where, and so many
people all looking
the same with only
their eyes uncovered.
The light hurt her,
and she could see the
person who was
holding her and wip-
ing her dry when she heard a voice announce, "It's a boy!"

Wrong! She thought. Wrong! She knew. She started to
yell and argue, but all she could hear was her crying getting
louder and louder.

"Hello! There has been a mistake here. It is not a boy! I am a girl!" She knew that she knew, and had known all along. Why would they say something as silly, as wrong as, "It's a boy"? How could they not know what was so obvious to her?

As her eyes got more accustomed to the light and the people stopped poking and prodding her, she looked down between her legs, and her cries got even louder. This is just so wrong, she thought, as she noticed what was there. How can a mistake like this happen? She tried to yell and explain that they were all so very, very wrong.

No one heard her. Not a single person could understand her. It was so clear and she was trying as hard as she could to let them all know that they were wrong, but once again she knew; she knew that they did not understand. She wondered if they would ever understand what a mistake was being made. All the people in the room seemed so happy as she was wrapped up in blue swaddling blankets. She cried and she cried. She wailed as loud as she could, and no one understood.

She was hearing voices both from inside and out. She realized she was not alone in here as so many other voices were also alarmed by what was happening. One voice was telling her that it would be OK, as another one yelled, "No way is this OK!" Another could not understand why no one would listen to her, as yet another was trying to figure out how to get them to understand. One was telling her that she was wrong, and that she really was a boy. She did not care very much for this voice. She heard a quiet voice in the back just crying and feeling helpless. She could really relate to this one. There was a consensus forming that this was most assuredly going to suck! She continued to cry.

She was placed on top of someone—her mom, and even as she was crying as loud as possible, she could feel the old rhythm—Ba–Bmmm...Ba–Bmmm...Ba–Bmmm. This was familiar, and she had to admit to herself, comforting. It was not as loud as it used to be, but she knew it was part of her world. She found herself gasping for air between her cries, and then suddenly found herself suckling on the offered breast. She could taste the sweetness of the offering and noticed her breathing slow down. As she slowly faded off into sleep, she could hear many of the clamoring voices inside of her, arguing, worrying, being angry, the ones feeling that they are not being understood and the one who steadfastly knew who she really was. They all knew that even though this first journey had been hard, it would be nothing compared to what was in store for her in the future.

This is when she knew that all the other inner voices were going to be right. She thought hard. Really, really hard. Just before sleep overtook her, she understood she had only one choice. She hid! She hid for a long, long time.

I Am

¹³ Moses said to God, "Suppose I go to the Israelites and say to them, 'The God of your fathers has sent me to you,' and they ask me, 'What is his name?' Then what shall I tell them?"

¹⁴ God said to Moses, "I AM WHO I AM. This is what you are to say to the Israelites: 'I AM has sent me to you.'"

¹⁵ God also said to Moses, "Say to the Israelites, 'The LORD, the God of your fathers, the God of Abraham, the God of Isaac, and the God of Jacob has sent me to you.' This is my name for-

ever, the name by which I am to be remembered from generation to generation."

—Exodus 3:13-15

"I am what I am, and that's all that I am."

—Cartoon Character, Popeye

It is a bit startling to see the commonality between the God of Abraham, Isaac, and Jacob, and Popeye, the Sailor Man! The comfort and security of identifying oneself as "I am who I am" or "I am what I am" being sufficient seems daunting and challenging for most of us. It certainly is for me. Struggling for over sixty years with my gender identity, along with my many other identities, has made it seem that identity and simplicity do not co-exist.

How often do we define and introduce ourselves by what we do, or what we have? God and Popeye were clear that their sense of Being was enough. However, each of us has so many different aspects of ourselves—or what we may call identities. No wonder it gets confusing how to fill in the sentence:

I am _____!

I will try. Allow me to introduce myself!

I am a transgender woman. In the trans community, I would be classified as a post-operative transsexual woman.

My name is Grace Anne Stevens. It has been my name legally since March 25, 2011. This name is on my driver's license, my social security card, my U.S. passport, all my health insurance cards, all my tax returns, and all of my credit cards. All of these have the gender marker "F" associated with my name.

My birth certificate from New York still has my given name of Larnie Steven Rabinowitz, born on August 13, 1947, and an "M" under the "sex" marker. At this time, I have no sense of urgency or interest in having it changed. This may be confusing to some people, and I have friends who feel strongly about their desire to change all of their documentation, but for me, and in this moment, it is fine to leave the document as it is.

It is always a philosophical challenge to describe or define oneself. I do not think it matters whether you try a thirty-second elevator speech or you have chapters of autobiographical facts that convey the experience of who a person is. However, here are some of my factoids.

Things I have:
- A Bachelor of Engineering Degree in Electrical Engineering from The Cooper Union (1969)

- A Masters of Arts in Counseling Psychology Degree from Lesley University (2009)

- Three children and two grandchildren

Things I do:
- I have worked as an engineer, engineering manager, program manager for over forty years.

- I have worked as a mental health counselor in a substance abuse clinic.

- I have been a leader in the local (Massachusetts) transgender community since 2009.

- I have created training and speaking businesses where I train organizations, showing them how to deal with change, authenticity, and diversity, which includes but is not limited to gender variance.

Things I am (the order of this list is not really important):
- I am a woman.

- I am transgender.

- I am a parent and grandparent.

- I am a student.

- I am a teacher.

- I am a leader.

- I am a counselor.

- I am at peace.

Most of all, I am a human being. I am the same as you in many ways and different than you in many ways. I want to love and be loved. I want to hold and be held. I want to be free to be and grow to whatever my heart and mind desire to the best of my ability. I want the same for you.

I have learned that all the having and doing did not bring me to the place of being at peace. When I finally accepted that I was a woman, that I was transgender, that I did not know everything, and could not control everything, peace took root within me. For this peace to grow and survive, I must nurture it daily.

Hiding

I have my books
And my poetry to protect me;
I am shielded in my armor,
Hiding in my room, safe within my womb.

—"I am A Rock," Paul Simon

...She hid! She hid for a long, long time!

She thought it was safe to open her eyes. Four years old already and she understood that he had learned to walk and talk and laugh and play. She could see through his eyes, and hear through his ears.

She watched everything with a deep longing and was learning along with him. She stayed hidden and was very, very careful so that he would not know she was there. If he saw her, she knew it would be a disaster. This was hard for her, and she was thankful that there were a few parts—these were the old familiar voices, who were now her friends, that were with her since that first journey. They were happy in their new jobs to protect her. Each of them was also quietly learning everything that he learned, and staying ready if she ever needed them.

She got a little giddy and hopeful the day he asked Mom to paint his nails red. She watched, as he seemed to really enjoy this. However, when he went outside, the other kids made fun of him. As he cried, she went deeper inside, and hid once again.

They were eight years old. He needed to get glasses and was fuming when Mom made him get the frames that were the color of flesh. He yelled and cried that they made him look like a girl, and made him too sissy looking. He was not rough like the other boys; he did not know how to play ball, after all. Every time his father asked him to play, Dad always said he threw like a girl. *He* was getting tired of this and did not know where he belonged. I am not a girl, he kept telling himself. I am not a girl!

She wanted to yell and scream, yes you are. Yes, *we* are a girl, yes…yes…yes! There was a crazy mistake made! Her inner friends watching, were warning her not to do this, it wasn't time yet. No, no, no! Take it slowly, they offered. He needs to find his place. Be patient!

What about me, she argued? I need to find my place, too.

Her parts were scared and warned her that no one would understand. They knew, and sadly she also knew they were right. She listened to them, at least for now. She was not happy at all. All she could do was sit back, watch, and wait for the right time.

It was less than a year later when she could wait no longer.

He was in third grade. Mom got a job, and he got a key to the apartment. He walked to and from school, and still he did not know where he belonged.

He would come home from school and make himself a snack. He had learned how to make a few things by now, and then started his homework or watched TV. He could not wait until Mickey Mouse Club was on. He was infatuated by Annette. He was not alone; as she watched, she so wished that she could be Annette.

One day she took the risk. She wasn't sure how she did it, but she took control. She had him walk to Mom's closet and stare at the few dresses hanging there. She stared for a long time.

They were much bigger than she was but still.... He was scared and tried to argue with her, but she was stronger and took down a dress, and they put it on. It draped and dragged on the floor. She had to stand on the bed to see her whole length in the mirror above the dresser. She collapsed in joy. Her parts warned her that she needed to be careful and put this away before Mom and Dad came home. It was a start. She knew she could force him to do this. He struggled with it and became very confused, but he could not stop her.

Hormones were making them both crazy.

His body was changing in so many ways that neither of them really liked. He was learning what the word horny meant, and as his body responded in new ways, she yelled and kicked and screamed, but when he was like this, she knew she lost control.

Neither of them was satisfied, nor did they know what to do. It was a stalemate of sorts. She had to hide, as he moved on in the world, and pick her spots carefully. She learned to do this. It was better than nothing. However, neither she nor he felt complete. They were both getting increasingly confused.

He liked girls. They took his breath away and made his body tingle in so many places. But he knew something was wrong. Why did he like to put on his mom's clothes? Why couldn't he stop? He wasn't queer. He didn't like boys. God, no! How could he even talk to a girl? What would he say? What would he do? What if they found out?

He was sixteen when one night after going to see a high school singing competition he was walking home with a girl he really liked. He did not understand why he tingled inside whenever he saw her. He could not even begin to know where the tingling started and ended. He was scared and confused, but it felt so nice.

It was a really long walk, and they talked about their classes and their teachers. The girl started to talk about her dreams and then innocently and deeply asked him about what his dreams were. The question was an immense trigger and froze him in his steps. So this is what a deer in the headlights feels like.

The only thought in his head was controlled by *her* inside not by him. His brain was awash with the single dream to become a woman! Crazy, he thought (*she* smiled as *she* realized how easy it was to control that thought). It felt like forever before he recovered to talk about becoming an engineer.

The thought now lingered in his mind all the time. Impossible! Incomprehensible!

Girls were risky! NO! MAYBE? YES? What could he do? He knew he had only one choice of what to do.

He hid! He hid for a long, long time!

Hamlet (Said It Best!)

To be, or not to be: that is the question:
Whether 'tis nobler in the mind to suffer
The slings and arrows of outrageous fortune,
Or to take arms against a sea of troubles,
And by opposing end them? To die: to sleep;
No more; and by a sleep to say we end
The heart-ache and the thousand natural shocks
That flesh is heir to, 'tis a consummation
Devoutly to be wish'd. To die, to sleep;

To sleep: perchance to dream: ay, there's the rub;
For in that sleep of death what dreams may come
When we have shuffled off this mortal coil,
Must give us pause: there's the respect
That makes calamity of so long life;
For who would bear the whips and scorns of time,
The oppressor's wrong, the proud man's contumely,
The pangs of despised love, the law's delay,
The insolence of office and the spurns
That patient merit of the unworthy takes,
When he himself might his quietus make
With a bare bodkin? who would fardels bear,
To grunt and sweat under a weary life,
But that the dread of something after death,
The undiscover'd country from whose bourn
No traveller returns, puzzles the will
And makes us rather bear those ills we have
Than fly to others that we know not of?
Thus conscience does make cowards of us all;
And thus the native hue of resolution
Is sicklied o'er with the pale cast of thought,
And enterprises of great pith and moment
With this regard their currents turn awry,
And lose the name of action.—Soft you now!
The fair Ophelia! Nymph, in thy orisons
Be all my sins remember'd.

—*Hamlet* by William Shakespeare

Fifty years ago as of this writing (1964), I was a junior in high school. I was required to memorize Hamlet's soliloquy for my least favorite class, English. I'm not really sure how I did this while memorizing all the lyrics to the Beatles songs, as this was the time of the so-called British invasion, but I managed well enough to pass the test.

I was at the leading edge of giving up the "being" part of my life. The girl that asked me about my dreams was in my English class. I would tingle each time I saw her, but was afraid and confused.

"To be or not to be?" Today, we have data showing that the attempted suicide rate for transgender people exceeds 40 percent of those surveyed. This compares with the overall population attempt rate of around 2 percent. Being different, not understood, rejected for expressing one's truth in a culture that lacks understanding and acceptance, no doubt has created these "slings and arrows" that result in so many trans folk trying to opt out of living. My choice was to hide and "Bear those ills... Than to fly to others that we know not of."

Hamlet wrestled with this very question: to be or not to be? It was a choice of life or death. I am glad that I really did not care about English class at that time and never bothered to analyze what this all meant. I was happy to escape in my books, my math and science classes, TV and radio, and with a basketball. It was easier than I thought to stop feeling. I became numb to feelings.

As high school years morphed into college years, I already tuned out well before the summer of love, Timothy Leary, and the age of the hippies. I just locked myself up in my room and read and watched TV. I had tons of awareness of life—happening all around me—with little to no participation in it. That was enough for me. It was really nonbeing, non-feeling, and needless to say, I had no idea about relationships and friendships. Parts of me longed for these things, but the barriers were well set to not let anyone close. Lies, excuses, and denial were on autopilot. This was my life.

There is a construct that many people struggle with. It is the dilemma of Be-Do-Have. It is not very different than the old chicken and egg, which comes first question. I learned to live a life of Doing and Having. This was by me, and for me. Others were hardly a consideration. How I appeared to *Be* in the world was the result of acting a role I thought I needed to represent; a mask hid who I was inside from the world and also from myself. I had parts that were arrogant, controlling, obnoxious, and knew it all. There were the clever parts that could turn your words around against you. When I succeeded, there was a smug part that laughed and felt triumphant at protecting me from any close relationship. Each and every part feared that if anyone got too close to me and really knew me, the sky would come tumbling down. There were always a few voices that were pleading for connections to other people. They were always drowned out and pushed to the side by the parts that believed that this would not be safe for him. There was no way those protector parts would allow any connections to be made.

I wanted to avoid finding out and dealing with what was inside me. As you know now, I avoided this for decades. For most of my life I did not even know that this was my basic operating system. I thought it was just me being me! I believed the god-like "I AM WHO I AM" was sufficient and justifiable. I was afraid to face my truth let alone to address it or even have the remote thought that I could live it.

Truth or Consequences

The choice of not being comes at a cost. Not only did I not understand when it was pointed out to me, but I fought it and the people who dared to point it out.

The consequence of nonbeing was non-feeling. Even today, I am not certain if I would diagnose this as a form of anhedonia, the inability to find pleasure in experiences which are typically enjoyable, or whether there were just some very clever parts who could selectively avoid admitting the feelings that were in me. That is, each time a feeling surfaced, it was time to hide. It is interesting to look back on how I managed to hide without any external substances. I joke that my drug of choice was television. I now understand it was not a joke. When the game trivial pursuit came out, no one would play with me as I seemed to have a storehouse of 1960s trivial knowledge. Sadly, I thought this was cool and was fairly arrogant about it.

Relationships were foreign to me. Isolation was well known, but accepted, even celebrated. I still struggle with changing this. I failed at even trying to socialize as either male or female. Today, I work hard at learning many of the social skills that most people have acquired early in life. I am challenged every day. Changing gender physically has been much easier than changing gender socially for me. I dare to say that this is not that uncommon for those who transition later in life.

Being on guard and hiding is hard to unlearn. The parts that have spent decades protecting me from relationships, even if they have new jobs to do, are not far from the surface. Learning to feel and trying to understand what each feeling is, and then what to do with these feelings is often confusing. I avoided sharing the confusion and asking for help at all costs. It is still a challenge for me today, but as I work on it, it seems to be getting easier.

In Search of Me

I went to college from 1965 to 1969. I lived at home in Brooklyn and commuted on the subway to lower Manhattan each day. This pretty fully occupied all my time, which was OK to me, as it kept me well isolated and in my head. I learned how to read standing up in the subway cars, while being mostly propped up by the other wall-to-wall commuters. I used to keep a list of all the books I read each year. It was a personal competition to see how much I could read. After all, I had to make good use of those two hours a day on the trains. I am pretty sure that each of those years I averaged reading about one hundred books per year, mostly science fiction and spy novels. All great escapist fare, as I so wished I could be living any life but mine.

Getting close to my classmates was out for so many reasons. My life consisted of school, trains, and back to my room with my books, radio, and TV. And the life of those thoughts inside me....

He was a mess. He poured over the copies of *Playboy* magazine he got every month. He had a subscription and his mom thought this was fine, so he did not have to hide it. He knew there were so many other things that really were hidden.

He devoured each and every page and wondered what sex was all about. He knew the physical release—his body was out of control, which he knew she hated so much, and then he felt guilty. But he had no idea if he could actually ever be with a girl. He knew he would have trouble hiding the other part that was always present. He doubted she would stay hidden and let him be. Every time he looked at the pictures of the beautiful women, she was right there with him. Their thoughts were so different. He dreamed of being with them and holding them while she dreamed of being them. He knew it made no sense. It seemed so hopeless.

She was a mess. She still spent so much time hiding, and had no idea if it would ever change. Everything she got him to read about gender still made her feel like there was something wrong with her. She hated this. She knew she was exactly who she was. He was the one that really wasn't being true!

She still felt guilty during the times there was no one home and she would try on some of Mom's clothes. She was always on guard listening for the key. It was better than nothing, but not much. It seemed so hopeless.

I wasn't sure that I was going to make it through college. The first year I had ten classes and got all Cs. The second year I got a D in Physical Chemistry. How I hated that class, the teacher, and how I worried that I would flunk out. There were so many general scientific background classes before it started to focus on my major of electrical engineering. What a relief it was when I got to the classes I liked and actually did OK. I made it through to graduate in 1969. I accepted a job in the Boston area. I would be leaving, no longer living at home in New York, at last!

I decided that I would rent a house with three of my classmates who were also moving to Boston. I am not sure what I was thinking at the time, but pretty sure I did not know how to live on my own. I was also afraid that if I was on my own, she might just take over everything, and there was no way I could allow that to happen.

It was the summer of 1969. I left New York, the first man landed on the moon, Woodstock changed the world, and the New York Mets won the World Series. All major events!

It was all new and strange, and I really did not have anything to do with my roommates. I bought a TV, kept it in my room and watched it alone. At work there were many newly hired engineers, and a bunch of us became friends. This was new for me, and I had to be careful. Everything inside was under control as there was so much else going on. One year later, I decided to move. One other new friend and I decided we would get an apartment together. This arrangement also lasted only a single year.

It was 1971. For the first time in my life I would be living on my own. I was pretty clear that I was not very good at having roommates. I had no idea what it would be like living on my own, and had a bundle of worries, but I had to do it. It seemed that all my friends who were rooming together for the past year or two also went out at the same time to get their own apartments. Apparently being twenty-four was a time for all these techie types to figure out how to live on their own. I wondered if any of my friends had secrets they might be hiding, too.

He was torn. It was lonely. He wanted to find a girl, yes, definitely a girl, but had no idea how to, what to say, and even more scary, what to do with them. What if they asked him about his dreams? How would he handle it this time? His other friends were starting to date, and there were groups of girls that somehow started appearing around at parties. His friends started to rent ski lodges in the winter and beach houses in the summer. He joined them to not be so alone. Perhaps he is just a late bloomer, he thought and was OK with it. If only she would let him just figure himself out!

Glasses and bushy hair.

She really wondered if this would be her chance to get out. Her friends still told her to take it slowly. She finally understood them and was willing to do this.

She hated how he looked now. He was so hairy! She thought he grew this to spite her, she really did. She had a plan. The moustache would be the first thing that had to go. Once she was able to get him to get rid of it, she could work her way out some more. She was glad she had learned to be patient. She had a plan.

She really disliked the kinky bush of hair on his head. She walked up and down the aisles of the drug stores and found out where the home hair straightening products were. She remembered when her mom used to do permanents for some of the neighbors and thought this wouldn't be too hard to do. She wasn't quite sure how he would explain this change to others, but left that problem to him. After all, it was the seventies and there were glam rockers everywhere now. It was on a crisp Sunday morning in the fall of 1972 when she took over and executed the plan. He tried to stop her, but she was stronger—at last!

At first I was really embarrassed to go out with my hair changed. I bought my first hair dryer and figured out how to do some styling with it. The kinks were out but the natural waves were still around. This is true even today when I professionally straighten my hair. It has been over forty years since I have had the kinky, curly hair. I never miss it. Looking back, this was perhaps my first transformation. I survived it OK. Then contact lenses were added to create my new look. She then wanted some clothes.

Contacts and straight hair.

There were a number of these one-stop department stores around and I started buying a few items of women's clothing. I was a wreck each time I did and was thinking of one excuse after another. I never had to use any of them. I hid the clothes in a suitcase in my closet. She seemed to be happy...for now.

I started to date. I was somewhat able to keep my inner worlds separate. It was even more confusing when I was dating more than one girl at a time. I have no idea what I was thinking back then. And still more women's clothes filled the suitcase. As long as I gave her some space, there seemed to be a balance of sorts. I was still totally confused, but finding a way to manage all the different forces inside of me. I wondered how long I would be able to do this.

Part of keeping the balance was to make sure she could dress and relax just listening to music and reading. One evening she had taken over and was enjoying herself. She was dressed, along with makeup, and was relaxing with the stereo on, and then there was a knock on the door. PANIC! She shut the music off. The knocking continued. It was the girl who lived in the apartment directly above, knocking and asking to open the door, and she knew "he" was in there. Just like a deer in the headlights, I froze and did not know what to do. I never answered the door. My neighbor never knocked or talked to me again.

The next time she took over, she kept the music very low. She began to realize that she was not as isolated and safe as she thought she was and needed to always keep her guard up. For the first time she thought she needed some of the other parts that were doing this for him.

He was thinking of getting married, and preparing for the internal battle. He was hoping she would just go away and let him be, but really didn't expect this to happen. He was right.

A Life Well Lived or, Well, a Life Lived

five hundred twenty-five thousand
six hundred minutes
how do you measure — measure a year?

...in truths that she learned
or in times that he cried
in bridges he burned
or the way that she died

—"Seasons of Love," *Rent*, lyrics by Jonathan Larson

"Seasons of Love" poses a great question. How does one measure a day, a year, a life? I was married for twenty-five years, while internally a battle was being waged that no one but I was aware of. I operated from my head—from Doing and Having. Yet, I was far from whole, far from happy, even if I could let that feeling in. It is difficult to write about this as it is not only my story but involves other people whom I cannot speak for. I also respect their boundaries more now than I used to.

I got married in 1976. I had lived alone in a small studio apartment between 1971 and 1976. Over the five years that transpired, I acquired a few suitcases of women's clothes that I would often wear in the evenings. In 1976, I purged all the clothes, with the not uncommon, but incorrect, feeling that this part of my life was over. Yes, I thought that being married would put an end to the internal struggle.

She was a little concerned but knew that she was not going anywhere. She had mixed feelings about throwing away all the clothes that were in the suitcase. Most of them did not fit right and really were not very nice. It was so hard to have him shop and not be able to try anything on. So much of the mail-order clothes just did not look the same when she put them on. None of the shoes they bought ever fit either. Why did women's shoes never come in sizes bigger than ten? He wore a man's ten but found the women's tens were so painful to get on, let alone walk in! She needed a woman's size twelve shoes, but had no idea where to find them. It was exasperating!

It was harder throwing out some of the clothes she had made for herself. Mom gave her an old sewing machine in 1972, and she taught herself how to sew. It was fun buying fabric and patterns and the engineer parts enjoyed figuring out how to make things fit. She became good at sewing and ripping and resewing. In 1974, she was so excited when she bought her own brand new sewing machine.

She even made some clothes for him. After all, it was the seventies and leisure suits were in! Sewing as a hobby was even something he talked about and found that it was a great conversation topic with girls. This often confused her but she could tolerate the talk.

Even before their engagement, he volunteered to make clothes for his girlfriend. She was OK with this. The Doing parts were so happy even if the Having parts felt a bit deprived. She realized that she was having a wonderful vicarious experience in making clothes—that she could never wear—for someone else. Surprisingly, she enjoyed this.

He was quite confused. He knew he felt something but really could not describe it, or put words around it. He was afraid, and was being torn up inside. Was this love? Was this what it was about? He did not know and had no idea how to find out. He really liked his girlfriend, her energy, and the way she looked and felt. Her smiles made him tingle—that old feeling again.

There was that American Dream thing he had deep inside, too. Growing up in Brooklyn in a two-room apartment until he was twelve and then moving to a four-room apartment where he lived until he graduated from college at twenty-two, he wanted a house and a place to put up his very own basketball hoop. He so wanted that!

He could get that and more and that would be fine, right? People get married all the time. He was not sure why, but it seemed like the right thing to do.

He was listening to a fair amount of parts working very hard trying to hold back these feelings that were creeping into the system. Their jobs were to block any and all feelings and had been pretty successful for years, but for some reason, they were starting to let some feelings through.

A part so lonely was getting louder and louder each day and seemed to be drowning out all the other voices inside him. This part was even drowning out her voice. She was getting frustrated, but as she watched all the turmoil in the system, she knew it was going to be another instance where she would need to gather her inner friends, the parts she knew she could trust, and prepare them all to hide once again. He was so confused that he only had a fleeting sense of the sadness in her. She always made him so crazy. Perhaps everything will be so much better if she does hide again, he thought. He and his inner friends had so much other work to do and big decisions to make.

We were married, moved into an apartment, and we both worked. When we raised the question of having a family, my Having part took control. The ultimatum was, "No family until we buy a house."

In 1977, we bought our first house and the family followed. Our first son, Simi, was born in 1978, a daughter, Stella in

1980, and another son, Elie in 1983. Oh, and of course, a dog joined the mix in 1979. A larger car accompanied each addition. The second and larger home came between the second and third child. Have, have, have was working and working well—or so I believed.

I was more surprised than anyone at how much I *loved* my kids! Yes, this feeling—it was love. It was inseparable from another feeling—responsibility. This was so new for me. I had no idea what to expect. I had never seen a baby being born, or ever thought about what being a dad would be like. I was in the hospital right after my son Simi was born, and when I saw him in the nursery, where there were rows of newborns, I was transported to another universe. Since that day in 1978, I have joked that my dream job would be a nurse in a hospital nursery. Cuddling and swaddling, feeding and comforting the newborns, and getting to smell baby all day long!

Walking the colicky infant at 2:00 a.m., as he did not sleep through the night for almost eighteen months, was my job. This was fine as there was no way my wife could have done it. Babies are so much work! Nursing mothers have days they do not get dressed! I never read that in any set of directions. No matter how challenged I was with feelings, I could not hide my empathy for what she was going through. Perhaps that is why I can honestly say I have not slept through an entire night in the last thirty-five years. But it was worth it. Changing diapers, tickling and razzing them, I loved it and them.

Do babies bring couples together or drive them apart? Parents have so much to do, and perhaps our innate internal drive to perpetuate the species makes the child more important than each other. What happens when the parents themselves are not fully engaged as part of the couple? Where do they spend their positive energies, and where do they get to express the negative ones? How many of us know about this before we get into it? I was clueless. I truly do not know if it would have mattered. We each focused on the children. We were (and are) great parents.

I suspect this is not uncommon. As parents, we seem to have a natural sense of responsibility to our children. How often does this sense overrule our responsibility to our partners? Do we really understand the balance of relationship with a partner when it is so much easier to be the boss, the one in charge of the relationship with a child? At least we may think this is the required parental role. I now recognize I did not even have a relationship with myself. My parts were constantly arguing and fighting, and I did not have the skills to reassure them that all would be fine. As different parts would overwhelm me and take charge, my relationship with my partner was never their first task. It usually was trailing well behind thoughts for the kids and myself. I was unaware of the consequences of this behavior for years. As part of a couple, I now know how much I did not provide for my partner.

Five hundred twenty-five thousand six hundred minutes. Twenty-five years. I do not even want to do the math. I did not know the song "Seasons of Love" until well after my kids fell in love with the musical *Rent* in high school. Even though I was aware there was a trans character in it, I had parts that were not ready to see it. Today I cannot listen to the music or watch the movie without boxes of tissues.

How do you measure, measure a year? How do you measure
twenty-five years of a marriage—a family—a lifetime? How do
you do this when one is hiding the entire time?

We would have been considered upper middle class, living in a well-off suburb and putting three kids through private
colleges, with a fleet of five cars at one point, but we did not
prepare or plan well and had no idea how to pay for it all. Parts
of me were in panic mode over money, but no one knew. To the
world at large, paying three tuitions would appear as a huge
success. I had worked at multiple high-tech start-ups, none of
which were successful. Jobs came and jobs went, and there were
stints of joblessness. These were the wretched, worrisome in-
between times that many people experience. We were not im-
mune to hard times. However, I was at a larger company during
the dot-com explosion and luckily left before the bottom fell out.
I made some money off of the stock and was able to pay all the
bills, all the debt. I look at this as one of the many blessings in
my life. I once thought that if I could pay the bills, I could leave
the marriage. I even stated it in anger and despair. My marriage
did not survive. At the time, the break up did not feel like a
blessing. I did not have any idea what was next for me.

I was hiding, and had little to give. I thought I gave so
much, but it was the doing and having parts that were giving. I
was drained. Without being, I had nothing emotional to provide
to my spouse. I had nothing to give to myself either, and I think
this was finally taking a toll on me. What was a tolerable life had
approached being intolerable. We could argue, or fight, or blame
each other for not taking responsibility and fixing it. In fact, we
often did. I can only speak here for my internal battles, and I

know at the time, I was not able to fix them, let alone repair anything outside of me.

While from the outside our life continued to look well lived, it did not feel well lived from the inside.

To outsiders, I am sure it looked like, "A Life Well Lived."

To me, it was just existing, or, "Well, a Life Lived."

...And Then I Was Alone

I have so many different personalities in me, and I still feel lonely.

—Tori Amos

She was getting very excited. She knew that there was so much about to happen, and although there were so many parts running around in various stages of panic, in about a month, she would be able to take a giant step forward. Many of the parts begged her to keep away from everything that was about to occur, as it was not about her now, and there were so many possibilities for things to go really badly. She had been so patient for so long, and knew the pain that she had been through, so she agreed to stay far back during the next month.

He was scared and worried. He knew he wasn't alone as the background chatter was deafening. The only thing he knew for sure was that everything was about to change. All his planning parts were noisily busy and preparing for the worst possible outcomes. There were parts in the background that were sad and angry and lonely and arguing with each other. There were others whimpering and crying in the back somewhere, as they moved further and further away. There was no turning back. It was impossible to continue as it had been. This was absolutely clear, and had been clear for some time. This did not make it any easier as he continued to worry.

They both were making me nuts! Who the heck was in charge here? The decision was years coming, yet it was so incredibly difficult.

It was June 2001. My oldest son graduated from college and was living at home. My daughter finished an entire college year in Strasbourg, France. My youngest was about to finish off his senior year of high school and was wrestling with the choice of performing in a jazz concert or the baseball playoffs (baseball was the choice). The kids and I had a two-week road trip planned to the Midwest for the middle of June. I had an apartment rented for July 1, and it was time to tell them that Mom and Dad were getting divorced. I was worried for all sorts of reasons and wondered if the road trip would happen.

Usually when a family meeting is called, it seems everyone there is ready for the bad news that will follow. This one fit the bill. We gathered around the kitchen table. Not one of the five of us was smiling. I looked at my wife and she right back at me with the piercing look that said, "You tell them!"

I don't remember the exact words I used, something about how they knew that Mom and Dad were not getting along well and we decided that we would be splitting up. I would be moving out.

Silence.

Our oldest son and daughter went directly up to their rooms on their own while the youngest sat and talked for a bit.

My wife went up to see our daughter, and I went to see our son. His first words to me were totally unexpected.

"I am so glad you are doing this. I can't stand how you two are fighting all the time," he said.

I was speechless and did not know what to make of this. I can't remember what we talked about, but he still wanted to go on the road trip. The other kids did too. I am not sure how long it took for the shock of the announcement to pass and what became the new normal to begin. Dad would be moving out and from the kids' perspective, nothing else should change. It seemed like it would work.

I did not fall into the abyss quite yet.

Road Trip

Two weeks in the car with my three, now adult kids, with their about-to-be-divorced father was more of an adventure than we originally planned. The kids did a good deal of the planning for the trip. I am not quite sure how after being born and raised in Brooklyn, and hardly ever traveling out of New York City until after college, I raised kids who love the outdoors. I had just purchased a Toyota 4Runner, and I had a part that was excited to take it off-road, while a chorus of other parts were issuing warnings that I was way, way over my head in thinking I could drive in the woods.

The kids created the itinerary. It seems that they also have many planner parts inside of them too. It was a mix of baseball and camping.

They planned a two-week journey where we would start by driving from Boston to Cleveland and catch a baseball game at (what was then) Jacobs field. I added a request for a trip to the Rock and Roll Hall of Fame while we were there.

Then to Wisconsin for camping and kayaking out to the Apostle Islands in Lake Superior. On to Minnesota and canoeing at Boundary Waters with perhaps a plan to portage the canoes. Then looping back down through Iowa and visiting the Field of Dreams, and On to Chicago and Wrigley field to see the Cubbies.

I had many parts wondering if I (and we) would survive all this and what my life would be like when we returned. They were right at the surface: watching, watching, watching.

And then it was time to hit the road!

Wet Escape

I was *the* Dad! I was the one in charge of this trip, right? Even though my three kids were all adults, wasn't I the one who was supposed to be in charge, in control? Being in control was always so important to me for so many reasons.

This was the trip with just my offspring and me. This was different than the previous family vacations with Mom, Dad, and the kids. It seemed like a rite of passage. Perhaps it marked the end of family—well at least as we had known it. Or perhaps it marked a new beginning for each of us in a new type of relationship still to be defined. It was long, and for the first time in my memory, there were times that I neither drove nor sat in the passenger seat of the car. My part that wanted control was in panic mode. One after another, each kid said, "Dad, chill out!" It took me almost the entire two weeks on the road to get there. Yes, a new relationship with each of them was beginning.

The road trip was delayed a day as my son Elie's baseball playoffs continued to the state semifinals. I had mixed feelings when his team lost, but then our road trip could get under way. For one of our first stops on the trip, we had bought tickets for a baseball game at Jacobs Field in Cleveland, but having left a day later than planned, we missed the game. We did go to the Rock and Roll Hall of Fame. I am pretty sure that I enjoyed the trip down the rock-and-roll memory lane more than the kids did.

We left Cleveland and were heading north though Michigan to the Upper Peninsula usually referred to as the U.P. It would be the first night of camping, and the plan was to take the new four-wheel drive truck through a fifty-mile backwoods road just because we could. The talk in the car was to watch out for the "militias" who lived in the woods and would shoot first if you entered their territory. My Dad-in-Charge part was overwhelmed with fear. Stay cool; stay calm; nothing will happen. Every bump on the road instilled more fear. Those few hours through woods drained me. We made it through the back roads OK and saw some gorgeous areas on the way, but little did I know, the worst was still ahead of us, and my stress level was already heightened.

We had a plan. We were going to rent sea kayaks and paddle out about six miles to a backcountry campsite on Sand Island in the Apostle Islands. We had made our reservations for the kayaks, and the required training and the campsite long before. The kids were excited, although I was consumed with fear. I dared not show it. I was the dad, right! I am not a fan of water sports. I am not a good swimmer. I think part of the reason for this is that I could not see a thing without my glasses on and most of the time in the water I was without them. At least that is how I rationalize it to myself.

We made it to the kayak rental place. We were told to put on wetsuits. It is true, Lake Superior is never warm, and a wet suit is required. This was a first for me.

Our safety test to operate the kayaks was fairly simple—up to a point. Learning how to get in and attach the protective skirt was straightforward and mechanical. No biggie! I was dreading the wet escape test. Stella and I were in a two-person kayak, as were the boys in another. The test was to capsize your kayak, of course, holding your breath—and once underwater, pull the skirt release which then allowed your life jacket to "suck" you out of the boat and pop you up to the surface where you must proceed to right the kayak, climb back in, find the manual pump and pump out the water in the bottom of your kayak. The maneuver is called a wet escape. Once you can escape, they will rent you the kayak and wish you fun on your journey. Simple!

I was desperately trying to find a part of me that thought this was fun. Perhaps it wasn't too late to go back to the woods in the Upper Peninsula and look for the militia—that would be more fun than a wet escape.

I watched the others in the group take turns flipping their boats and popping out of the water. A few of them asked to do it over and over as they said how much fun it was. I watched Simi and Elie flip their kayak and pop up with smiles on their faces. I felt myself fading out of the present reality. Now, I know that it was a part of me that thought, "Any place else would be better than where I am right now." I was drifting away when the instructor said it was our turn. I am not certain which part nodded that I was ready and then Stella, who was in the front seat start-ed to rock the kayak back and forth. I heard her start to count—or did I really?

Rock to the left, rock to the right. "One."

Rock to the left, rock to the right. "Two."

Rock to the left. It was too late. Where am I? What am I supposed to do?

Rock to the right. "Three." Oh, crap!

I froze. I forgot to take a breath! We continued to rock to the right then hit the water. Even with the wet suit on, the first thing I noticed was the cold, the piercing cold. I wanted to yell and needed to breathe. I was underwater and opened my mouth. I was starting to choke, and somehow, from somewhere deep inside, a part was trying to get in control and get me out. It reached forward, fumbling in the dark, cold water, not looking, not seeing, but found the cord at the front of the skirt and pulled. I felt myself being sucked out of the kayak and popped to the surface both choking on the water I swallowed and gasp-ing for air. My embarrassed parts were there and ready to jump up once they knew I was safe.

My Dad-in-Charge part was looking for someplace to hide. As I popped up, I knew that everyone was looking at me and worrying. I had a worried part also, that I failed the kids and ruined the trip. Stella swam over to me as I rested on the capsized boat while I caught my breath. She was able to flip the boat, with only a little help from me and then helped me climb in first, still gasping a bit for air as I coughed and worked on clearing my lungs. Needless to say, the adrenaline was pumping wildly through me. Stella climbed in the boat easily, and we found the pump and cleared out some of the water in it. I think the instructor had pity on the old man, passed us, and said we were good to go.

This was only day three of the road trip, and I almost died. Right in front of my kids. I cannot even count the parts that were panicking and criticizing me. I wanted to cry, but I could not.

Then it got really scary.

We were bussed along the coast of Lake Superior to our launching point and left off with the kayaks. We had our tents and backpacks and food supplies stowed away in the hatches. It was a beautiful, calm day, and the surface of the lake was flat; no waves, no swells, and just a gorgeous afternoon to be kayaking on Lake Superior. We sea kayaked about six miles out to the north side of Sand Island. We enjoyed the trip and marveled at how beautiful it all was, even though I was a bit quiet and cautious due to my morning's near-death experience. We had a one-day supply of food as our plan was to camp in the wilderness for one night and return the next morning.

That night it started to rain. It was one of those infamous Lake Superior storms. We awoke in the morning and walked down to the beach to see what we should do. At that moment I did not realize that we were on the north side of the island and the storm winds were coming from the east. We noticed the choppy waters which now petrified me, but the kids all wanted to try to paddle back to the mainland. I think that my Dad-in-Charge part wanted to show he was strong and tough, or perhaps it was some other part, as I refused to listen to the clamoring inside me that it would not be safe to get out in the water. We packed up all the gear into the kayaks and agreed to leave. It was raining and choppy, and my daughter and I found we could not even turn the kayak into the waves once the boys pushed us off the beach. We almost flipped right back on to the beach. Fear took over as I yelled, "No, we are not doing this." We could not get the kayaks off the north side of the island, which a few hours later I realized surely saved our lives. I had everyone unpack and set up the tents again as we tried to figure out what to do.

A few hours later we were cold and hungry, and I decided to walk to the ranger's area on the southeast corner of the island. It looked like it was about three miles. As I hiked for help, I stopped at the east side of the island and watched what were ten-foot swells. I had never seen anything like this. The park ranger from the other side met me half way as he was called from where we rented the kayaks and told that we did not return. He kindly took me back to his cabin and gave me some food so we could make it through another night camping out.

On the second day of being stranded, the winds continued and they officially stopped shipping on Lake Superior. I hiked across the island again and asked the ranger to call for a ferry to get us off the island. I did not care how much it would cost. We left the kayaks beached high up in the sand near the woods, and we packed all our gear and hiked the three miles across the island to the dock.

I am neither a good nor happy bad weather camper. But, I did get quite a story from it.

I used to listen to the old Gordon Lightfoot song, "The Wreck of the Edmund Fitzgerald" about a ship on the Great Lakes that went down in a gale.

Now I truly understand what that was all about.

Not even a week gone and I'd had two existential experiences already. What a trip this was. Something changed in me; in fact, I think in each of us. A good, seemingly life-or-death adventure can take your mind off of an upcoming divorce. Now the kids and I had a great story to talk, joke, and exaggerate about and bond with that took all our minds off of the uncertain future.

On to Minnesota and up Highway 61 (so this is where Bob Dylan was from) to Boundary Waters. We changed our plans to canoe, portage, and camp as we felt that we had enough unknown adventures for a while. We met my son's friend who worked at Boundary Water Canoe Area for the summer, and he showed us the kitchen area where a bear had recently broken in and created havoc. Apparently there are many adventures in this part of the country. We canoed around but just for the day. We opted for safety. The kids did not fight me on this. A hotel was a welcome sight as was a good restaurant. We were glad that it was also a brewery.

We drove and talked and slept. We headed south through Iowa and went to Dyersville, to the Field of Dreams, the baseball field in the movie. They built it, and sure enough we came. After all, what is a baseball trip without it? We were ready with all our gloves, bats, and balls in the car and all played ball there for a few hours.

She was quiet and hiding for the past few days, but here at Field of Dreams she let me know she wanted something. She has been dreaming, since the day she was born, to be free; she told me. I knew this was true. I did buy her an oversized baseball shirt that she could use as a nightshirt that had Field of

Dreams on the front. This made her happy, and she went back deep inside.

Back through Chicago and we saw the Cubbies at Wrigley Field. We walked along the river and to the Navy Pier. We decided we could drive home from Chicago back to Boston in a long single day. We were packed and left the downtown hotel at 6:00 a.m. With the four of us taking turns driving, the eighteen-hour ride was one, long drive home, and my Dad-in-Charge part realized he no longer had to do that job. Sitting in the back seat, I saw each of my kids as competent adults, with their strengths and weaknesses, but they did not need a proactive dad to protect them any longer. Dad would and could be there for them if they ask. I also became aware that over the past week, I learned to take their advice to "chill." The second week of the trip had been more spontaneous, less planned, less controlled. The Dad-in-Charge part was also willing to find a new job. He was becoming Dad-the-Friend not only to my kids, but to the rest of my system as well.

Two weeks on the road with my kids. Awesome, and as in the ad, priceless!

A week later I moved out of the house. It was the July Fourth weekend. I was officially alone. For the first time in twenty-five years, I was not living with one, two, three, or four other people and a dog, that I called family. I was alone.

She could not remember feeling this happy. She was going to get clothes, lots and lots of clothes and make him dress up all the time. She could buy wigs and shoes and breast forms— yes real breast forms, and not have to worry about where to hide

them. This was her place now. She did not have to share it with
anyone. She'll take pictures—lots of pictures. It was going to be
her time. There was no way he could stop her. Why would he?
He did not have to worry about being caught, and she thought
he liked it, too. She was so happy.

   The kids helped me move. I felt so lucky. I slept on the
floor the first night, and then Stella and her best friend came
with me to buy a futon, and we packed it in the truck. They
helped me put it all together.

   I went to work each day, and for the next six weeks, each
night was a shopping spree to furnish the two-bedroom apartment I rented that was only one exit up the highway from the
house. My doing and having parts were also celebrating and
happy. I would go from store to store. I needed dishes, and sil-
verware, and pots and pans. I needed lamps and power cords,
bookcases and a computer table. I took some of the furniture
and an old TV with me. I brought my old sewing machine that I
had not used in many years, as we had bought a much higher
end one for my wife. I bought a new computer, monitor, and
printer and got online.

   Yes, she bought clothes also. This was new and strange.
Mail order was also much easier as I did not have to worry who
might find the package. Many years later I found out that this
was not true, as after I told the neighbors that I was trans, they
mentioned they always wondered why there were packages for
me from various women's clothing companies.

   I looked; I compared prices and always searched for the
best deal. It was interesting not having to discuss what someone
else might like. It was my choice only. It had been a long time

since I could just choose on my own. I had forgotten how to do this. It did come back.

I managed through the days at work. I was excited to know that each evening I would be out either on a scouting or purchasing trip. I was busy and had no time to think about where I was in my life or where I was going. After a long day and night and making some food and eating, almost each night, she appeared.

She, too, was happy.

For the moment there was no time to feel alone. This feeling did not last.

MAYBE?

Letting the Tears Flow

So take a good look at my face
You'll see my smile looks out of place
If you look closer, it's easy to trace
The tracks of my tears

—Smokey Robinson, "The Tracks of My Tears"

There is absolutely no doubt about it. It was an existential crisis. Long, long overdue!

It was August 2001. I was about to celebrate my fifty-fourth birthday. I was now officially separated and on the way to a divorce. I had my own two-bedroom apartment and much of what I needed to survive. She was buying clothes by mail order almost every night, and every now and then would risk buying something in a store. This made me a nervous wreck.

I completed all the shopping I needed to furnish my new apartment in about six weeks. There was no longer an excuse to go out and shop every night. I came home from work each night, and I was alone. There were no other people and concerns about what their needs and wants were in the moment. It was only me. Me, and all the different voices inside me. The questions at hand were who am I, what did I want, what did I need? Fifty-four years of hiding and the internal dialog and wars were all I now had. Internally, nothing much had changed. Externally, the distractions of being and interacting with and taking care of others were gone. What could I do?

I did the only thing I could. I cried and cried and cried.

I really did not even know how to cry. It is hard to remember the wash of feelings that flowed through me. My power of denial regarding my confusion about my own gender was deeply rooted, no doubt fueled by the cultural bias that only a clear binary division based on anatomy was acceptable. I was in fear, isolated, confused, on so many levels. These feelings were overwhelming me, and as I sat in the evenings, even with a different woman's outfit on, it seemed that my brain was shorting out. At that time, life was an unsolvable paradox for me.

I want to be with someone.

How can I do this if I continue to hide?

How can I be with someone if I do not hide?

Why am I like this?

What does this mean?

I am attracted to women.

I want to be a woman?

What am I?

How can I live?

These questions played over and over in my mind. I could not stop them. My head pounded. Until I let the tears out. The tears were not alone. There was the gasping for air. There was the snot dripping from my nose. For some reason I knew that I was not supposed to use tissues, and let whatever flowed out of my eyes and nose drip across my face and on to my clothes. I did not hear the TV or radio that was in the background as I cried and cried.

I have no idea if the way I remember this is true. My memory is that I cried for hours. I repeated this for days and then weeks. It may sound crazy, but the crying reached a point that it almost felt like an assignment; that I needed to go home and cry each night and see where it would take me. I did not realize it then, but it seems there was a part of me that thought crying was a good way to protect me from letting her completely take over my system. Perhaps that worked, but there was a more important—no let's call it a major—impact from all the crying.

I learned how to feel.

Now, this change did not happen all at once. I cannot even say how or when I even became aware of something changing in me. Perhaps it was a logical part—there sure were plenty of these in my system—trying to understand what the crying was all about.

"Crying was a response to something," the logical part argued to any other parts that were listening. Sure, there were questions that did seem to have answers, but life has been like that forever. I'll call that logical part the Scientist, and he was observing the crying for the hours, days, and weeks, and was so trying to figure out what was going on. He had one of those eureka moments and realized that my system was not stuck without answers to all the questions that were rolling around over and over. It was that the system either did not want to know or did not like the answers it was coming up with and the implications of those answers. The system felt that some of the answers might lead to the end of the system. The end of the world as I knew it. I never had a serious thought of suicide during this time, but I can say on occasion the thought, "Can I go on?" passed through me.

When the Scientist part watched me cry, he saw sadness, grief, and fear, mixed with a joy of releasing so much energy that was inside of me. He also observed a sense of wonder as I started to act like a kid in the candy shop, trying out each new flavor of feelings.

The questions I had were not being answered to any resolution, but an entire new sense of awareness was now being birthed within me. This awareness was being OK with my feelings and seeing what they felt like. I was still alone and isolated. The situation could not get any worse. Perhaps exploring this world—which I avoided my entire life—would lead somewhere different. I knew that crying would be part of this path and would not be easy to travel.

I started to become conscious of how I reacted to things all around me, to conversations at work and with others. I risked sharing some of my feelings with others to see if I even had the correct words and language. I was often at a loss on how to express what was going on inside of me. I had many parts scrambling trying to figure out boundaries where I could say something that would not give away too much information about my struggle with gender. Luckily those parts were all up for the task.

Going to movies now was so different than before. I let myself cry at movies. I could not believe how easy it was to just let go. In fact, I could not even control it anymore. I would keep my arm in front of my face so I could wipe the tears on to my sleeve. I still did not want anyone to see me. Many times I stayed in my seat until everyone left the theater. Crying and feeling was starting to be part of my life. It was fine if the tears flowed. Even though I did not know what was ahead for me, the tears were OK. Really.

The Big Closet

She quietly watched as all the crying occurred. She knew these feelings herself, as she had done so much crying all the times she was hiding. But now, she understood that there were so many other parts making themselves known that it would be best if she just watched from the sidelines. She had become very good at watching over the past fifty years. Some of the parts she saw she knew well, and found she was happy for them, too, that they could come out and be seen and heard. Some parts were new to her, and she was curious as to what they were all about. She did not know if they would be OK with her own plans now, or whether she might end up in a confrontation with them. She did have her plans, and now that there were no other people to share her living space—even her *being* space—with, she could wait a little longer. While she watched the crying, she was happier than she could ever remember being.

It was somewhat strange for me as I started to explore feelings. I so prided myself in being able to respond to people before they ever finished a thought or a sentence. I often interrupted them with the answer and was clueless why they did not respond to my perceived cleverness, which my arrogant parts usually defined as intelligence.

I could hear those arrogant parts chuckling and patting themselves on their backs with an "attaboy, you sure showed them up," comment. It took a good deal of internal effort to hold them back as I started to listen not only to the words that people were sharing with me, but also the way in which they talked, the emotions, the feelings they had. I wanted to touch these feelings, explore them, and try them on for size. I had so little idea how to do this. Sometimes I succeeded, and sometimes the old parts just did their thing.

Bit by bit, day by day, I had a chance to try on new feelings. I had a part that wanted to get this done with, but over time this part also learned to chill out and has taken on the job as the Feelings Explorer and has agreed to work as a consultant on an as-needed basis. We have become good friends and sometimes just get to chat. I am always in wonder that there are so many feelings to explore, and look forward to each opportunity that arises.

He thought that he was doing a pretty good job. It wasn't easy being caught in the midst of all that crying, and he was smack in the middle of it all. He understood that it was a crisis, and although it happened without him being prepared, he knew it had to occur. In hindsight, he knew there really was not any way to prepare for it. If he knew the crisis was coming, he would have worked so hard to avoid it.

The weeks he spent releasing were good even if there weren't solutions to every problem. All the energy he used to spend holding everything in was let go during those weeks of crying. He learned that he could ease up on the control of that— no, not let go completely, but he could ease up. He was still confused and struggling to figure out where he fit in the grand scheme of it all and what he should be doing. But somehow he felt less alone—no, not with other people, but just in his head. He had to learn more about all these feelings. He had to!

Once the crying abated, she did want to build out her wardrobe. She thought now that nothing would stop this.

The closets were beginning to fill up with women's clothes and shoes. Especially shoes. There was so much trial and error in mail-order shopping. I had not found a great supplier of women's size twelve shoes and went through many size eleven returns. But they were mine, and I had a place to put them. The previous year I worked out each morning at 5:00 a.m. with both weights and on an exercise bike and was the thinnest I had been in years, as I weighed about 150 pounds. I must have looked emaciated and will probably never get back to that weight. Trial and error taught me that my broader male shoulders required a woman's large size for tops, although I could generally fit into size ten skirts. Much more trial and error went into buying dresses. Depending on the dress, I needed a twelve or fourteen. I learned that finding the right size is a challenge for many women, and to never be surprised that the way clothes looked on the models in the ads and pictures I saw was nothing like how they looked on me.

Each day when I returned home from work, I was so excited to see if a new package had arrived. When one did, I could not wait to run up the flight of stairs to my apartment and open it. I laid each item out on the bed and had to choose what to try on first. Any troubles or issues of the day were forgotten so quickly as she completely took over, fully absorbed in what was taking place. Even if I had parts that had other commitments, they most often lost this battle of priorities. The few times they won, she was so upset and could not wait to get us all home so she could see what she would look like. That made the waiting time quite uncomfortable, as she thought of excuse after excuse to leave and get home.

Mirror, Mirror on the Wall

I considered myself a cross-dresser. Apparently she knew better than this, but at the time really did not care how I perceived the situation. Deep down I also knew that it was so much more than just the clothes, but there was no way for me to admit or accept that thought. After all, if it were anything more than cross-dressing, what would I do? It was all so impossible—for so many reasons. Not now, not ever. All so impossible!

I lived in the Biggest Closet I could ever dream of. My apartment had two bedrooms and plenty of closet space. I purchased dressers just for her, and it did not take long

Living in the Big Closet.

before there were more women's clothes than men's clothes. However, she never went outside. Oh, no! That was still beyond any realm of possibility. No one could know, no one could see.

Impossible! How could I ever explain or live with this if someone found out? *There is no way!*

I hung a full-length mirror at the end of the hallway. I could parade down the twenty feet or so and see myself in the latest outfit. I purchased makeup for the first time and played with it, having absolutely no idea what I was doing. I purchased real breast forms for the first time. Yes, real silicone. This was such a jump from stuffing a bra with socks or even homemade sand bags made by filling up pantyhose with sand. Perhaps I was a bit obsessive compulsive in my acquisitions and my fantasy world of dressing up almost each night.

Dressing this way was exhilarating for me and relaxing.

Taking pictures dressed.

However, something was missing. It was OK to be dressed and sit around, and I found myself constantly walking over to the mirror. She needed to see herself. She needed proof that she was there. Even when I took some pictures I was so scared to have the film developed. Who would see these pictures? What if I was questioned? What if they were stolen? I risked these possibilities a few times, but the results were usually pretty bad, and the experience was gut wrenching each time.

She needed mirrors and pictures to validate her existence. It worked for her, and it also made a difference to me, no matter how crazy this may sound. Pictures of me dressed in women's clothes was not only a proof of existence, it was a cause for hope for us all. Perhaps someday this will be how I am in the world. Everything I knew told me of the risks, the costs, the losses, and the impossibilities, yet being able to see her let me enjoy the fantasy—at least momentarily.

It took some time before I purchased a digital camera. Oh, how her world changed! Pictures were now unlimited, and there was no middleman to worry about. I could easily access a color printer and photo paper. There were small tripods for these cameras, and I learned how to shoot in a few areas of my apartment. These pictures were only for me and for her, of course. I could see them on the computer but I also printed them all. I still have a file full of them. Some are good, and some are, well, not so flattering.

Each new outfit arriving required taking a picture. I hardly had a chance to enjoy one outfit when it was time to try another. Even I thought, there was something wrong with this behavior, but I could not stop the parts that were doing this.

Pictures were validating. They were a proof of existence.

As the Internet grew, there were more and more websites by cross-dressers with pictures posted. At the time, there was no way I would post my own pictures, but at least I knew I was not the only one out there that may have had this behavior. Now I was not alone!

I took pictures for years. It was very important to me. Perhaps I was just an old man in a dress, but it made me feel good, and again, it helped me know that she was there, she was part of me—or perhaps even more!

It is interesting to look back now and notice that since my transition, I take much fewer pictures. It is nice to have pictures, and yes, they still provide some softer and milder sense of validation to me; more like yes, you did it! I am now validated each day by being my true self.

The mirror still hangs on the wall in the hallway. Each morning as I walk naked from my bedroom to the shower, I look and see my body—yes, my body that is now aligned with my brain. Pictures are nice and were needed at one time, but are needed no longer.

The validation is now internalized, and there is not a moment that goes by when I do not feel the blessing about being me.

When the Student Is Ready

Unconscious.

Alone.

Not really so alone in my head. All the chattering, all the thoughts, all the voices were present. All the crying seemed to birth the new voice of "the kid in the candy shop" who wanted to try on feelings of different sorts. Now I am pretty sure that this new Kid-in-the-Candy-Shop part is really the old part that kept me unconscious, that has now been willing to take on a new task: explore feelings. That part sure seemed happier.

For so many years, Unconscious was protecting me.

I knew she was inside me. I even knew that she was me!

There was no way!

I knew I could not keep doing or living my life, without at least exploring more about me; why am I like this, and what can I do about it? How do I do this while still hiding from eve-ryone?

Was this crisis I went through enough for me to learn and even entertain the possibility of change? There is an old Bud-dhist proverb that is well known.

When the student is ready, the Master appears.

Was I ready to unlearn so much of the past? Were my parts open to taking on new tasks? How did I fit in this world? Who am I?

The only way I knew how to do anything about this was through books. After all, I did live by the belief that I was that rock, that island that had "my books and my poetry to protect me."

I again started to read. No longer was my reading a form of escape. No longer did the piles of books contain the latest sci-ence fiction adventure, or the latest thriller by Clancy or Lud-lum. My reading was a search for understanding. All my hiding, all my numbness to feelings, every part of me that held me back from Being had limited my views of claiming anything that I could believe in. I said earlier I was operating strictly by Doing and Having, and with that girl inside me, who wanted so much to come out, there was no way my parts would let that happen. I could not stay this way any longer. I had to look at my world— no, *the* world differently. So I started to read. Perhaps for the first time, I read with an open mind. I had no baseline other than hiding. It had to change!

As summer turned to fall, I read constantly, with an openness I never felt before. My resistance (yes many parts at work here) was falling away as there was a logical part remind-ing them all, that everything that was done before clearly was not working. Luckily, those resistant parts acquiesced, and I learned so much. I read about life, love, and relationships. It was not easy to look at myself through a new lens.

I found the journal that I kept during that time in my life. On the front page I had copied something from the *I Ching*. I am not certain which book I originally found this in, but it meant a great deal to me at that moment in time.

> *It is only when we have the courage*
> *To face things exactly as they are,*
> *Without any self-deception or illusion,*
> *That a light will develop out of events,*
> *by which the path to success*
> *may be recognized.*

I Ching, Hexagram 5, Hsu—Waiting (Nourishment)

While writing this book, I investigated the hexagram a little more and am shocked by the underlying meaning of the necessity of waiting to gain strength and nourishment. It took me another decade to gain the strength and courage to make the decision and take the action to live my truth. I suspect that this hexagram had more meaning to me than I even realized back then.

On the next page in the journal, I drew a box with the title and author of each book I completed during those three months. Here is the list of books that I read through the fall of 2001.

- *Living a Life That Matters*, Harold S. Kushner

- *The Road Less Traveled*, M. Scott Peck

- *Facing Codependence*, Pia Melody

- *The Power of Now,* Eckhart Tolle

- *The Art of Happiness,* The Dalai Lama

- *Excuse Me, Your Life is Waiting,* Lynn Grabhorn

- *A Return to Love,* Marianne Williamson

- *Illusions,* Richard Bach

- *Love and Survival,* Dean Ornish

- *Keeping the Love You Find,* Harville Hendrix

- *The Four Agreements,* Dan Miguel Ruiz

- *The Seat of the Soul,* Gary Zukav

- *When Things Fall Apart,* Pema Chodron

- *The Dark Side of the Light Chasers,* Debbie Ford

- *Spiritual Divorce,* Debbie Ford

- *In the Meantime,* Iyanla Vanzant

Perhaps this was an intense course in Life. I was still in my apartment through this time and alone. Even though I was dressed in women's clothes for almost all of this reading time—which made her very happy—I truly was open to seeing Life in a different way.

Somehow, through these readings, I found a new sense of a spiritual center. I am not sure how, but I gained an understanding or perhaps a belief in the interconnectedness of all things. My controlling parts that already were learning to chill were now beginning to accept this connection more and more and willing to become door openers for new thoughts and ideas. These books planted many seeds in me. However, the ideas were still only in my head. Going out into the world and acting, no, *being* different was another giant leap for me. Could I go out and deal with people in a different way and still protect the secret within me? I risked it, and it did not take long to get some feedback.

The feedback was from the kids. As I met them both individually and together whenever they were around, they remarked that both Mom and Dad were so much easier to get along with now. I shared about all the reading that I have been doing. They were interested in listening to me in a new way. I was no longer telling them how they should live. I was sharing that I was trying to learn how I should live. It is amazing to me that Elie tells me now that my actual transition to live female in 2011 was a less drastic change for him than the changes he saw in me in late 2001 to 2002.

For some reason she loved all the time reading. She was out, dressed, and felt so comfortable to not be buried so deeply inside. Many of the books really seemed to be focused on women's viewpoint, which she really liked. She remembered all the years, long ago, when she watched over everything that he was learning, so she could learn, too. It was so long ago, and it took her a little bit of time to realize there was now an opportunity for her also. She took in everything and wondered what it would be like if she was even more out in the world and meeting other people. What would she be like? Her old inner friends got a bit nervous when they heard what she was thinking. "It's still not time," they reminded her. She knew they were right, and was really enjoying the moment. She responded laughingly, "Hey, can't you let a girl dream a little?"

I needed to get out of my apartment and find more ways to learn. I saw notices for a weekend seminar on relationships. It was named, "Loving Yourself, Living Fully." The notice stated it was for singles and couples, and was based on the work of Harville Hendrix. I signed up, read the two required books (both on the above list) by Harville Hendrix and Pia Melody, and was ready for my first of what has turned out to be many experiences at a seminar.

I think that I was the only single person there. The room was filled with a good number of couples; all hoped to improve their relationships. Even the seminar leaders were a couple. They were both therapists and as it turned out were doing their own work while leading and demonstrating to the class.

The class focused on so many interesting topics, including shame, communication, lost and denied selves. Part of the time I was triggered back to my own marriage, and part of the time my Know-It-All part popped out, certain of what would be next. My protectors were on guard throughout the two days to make sure I did not reveal anything too secret.

I was hooked on all of the language and exercises. At this time, I had no idea my journey would lead me to a degree in counseling, no idea at all. At the conclusion of the seminar, a woman who was part of a couple that I had worked with handed me a flyer about another type of seminar she thought I might be interested in. I thanked her, glanced at it quickly, and put it in my bag and promptly forgot about it.

Apparently, the student was ready! At the very least, some parts were.

What Is True?

Oh, mirror in the sky, what is love?
Can the child within my heart rise above?

—Landslide, Stevie Nicks

Looking back to the end of 2001 there are times I wish I knew then what I can say I have learned so far.

Each day, our Truth is prepared to battle for its existence. It has no other task. It is tireless. No matter what the outcome of the previous day's battle, truth will come back once again to fight—to live—to be!

There are many enemies inside of us that will fight that Truth for every inch of ground. So many of us are taught or acquire the belief that our Truth will separate us from others when we so long for attachment. Our basic needs of wanting to be seen, heard, touched, and held seem to believe that Truth will make us too different, too unique—after all, we are like snowflakes—and that will be responsible for our separation from others.

> I have learned that Truth is not competitive.
>
> Our acceptance of others for who they are can create a better and stronger attachment and belonging than ever existed before. Accepting our own truth builds the nursery where love can grow.
>
> It is only when we have a loving relationship with ourselves, we can then have enough love to share and give to others. After all, we cannot give away what we don't have.

Only when we can accept our own truth and understand that our uniqueness, our individuality, and our sense of who we are does not need to separate us from others and when our identity does not need to be validated by others—when we truly know that we are enough, then, and only then are we comfortable for others to live in their own truth.

I have learned that Truth is not competitive.

Our acceptance of others for who they are can create a better and stronger attachment and belonging than ever existed before.

Accepting our own truth builds the nursery where love can grow.

It is only when we have a loving relationship with ourselves, we can then have enough love to share and give to others. After all, we cannot give away what we don't have.

In *The Road Less Traveled*, M. Scott Peck defines love as follows:

"The will to extend one's self for the purpose of nurturing one's own or another's spiritual growth."

When I hid my truth, I did not nurture my own growth. I denied it in so many ways. I am amazed at how many parts felt it was important to protect me from what was in me from the very start. How could this happen?

They both knew the battle was going on for years. She always knew who she was, even if from that day she was born, her body lied to her. That was her *nature*. She loved when she first heard the quote by Descartes, "Cogito sum ergo." She thought, therefore she was! She always knew what was true.

He, on the other hand, was always trying to figure out where he fit in and what he had to do to belong. He was so aware of all the messages that bombarded his senses all the time: be strong, be tough, don't cry! It seemed that every message was telling him, imploring him, *nurturing* him to be a certain way, to fit in. He so wanted to belong to something! Yet, he always thought that the risk of belonging was too high to take.

Life was an endless battle to him. She was always there, watching, lurking in the background and overwhelming him at every opportunity. His guards worked hard to stop her, and sometimes they succeeded. There were planning parts worried about what he would say or do if someone found out, or even questioned him about anything to do with sex or gender. He spent so much energy on this.

I was still struggling with trying to understand myself. I felt compelled to come home from work and dress, but there was no way I would ever consider leaving my apartment as a man in a dress. No way!

She was there! I knew it was true! I knew I had been denying her for so long.

We had been living in the four-room apartment, where I had my own bedroom, for a year. To me life was good, even though I already was struggling with that girl in me. It was just another Sunday morning. Dad already had gone for a walk to buy the newspapers and get some bagels, lox, and cream cheese. It was 1961, and this was still a weekly extravagance for us. We were what would best be described as a working class family, although I really had no idea of this at the time.

As usual, Dad came home with the *New York Daily News* and the *New York Daily Mirror*. This was a ritual seven days a week. At that time New York City had morning, afternoon, and evening newspapers to choose from. We were not a *New York*

Times family, no not at all. My parents and their families were working class survivors of the depression. I never knew we were (relatively) poor. Dad also had one more newspaper that was part of the usual Sunday package. This was the *National Enquirer*. My mom, dad, and I always enjoyed the crazy scandalous stories about both famous and ordinary people. This day, however, was different.

On most Sundays, I would grab the comics from both the News and Mirror as quickly as I could. I needed to keep up with Dick Tracy and Joe Palooka. I do miss these characters. I glanced at the front page of the *Enquirer* as the paper lay on the coffee table. It had a picture of a beautiful woman who at first glance I thought was Brigitte Bardot. Then the words froze me. The headline said something about sex-change and how she used to be a man! This picture was of Cocinelle, a French showgirl who had a sex-change operation in 1958 in Morocco, the story said. It took me a while to get my hands on this article when neither my mom nor dad was looking. The concept was new to me. People can and do change their sex. How could this be?

He made sure they were in the kitchen when he grabbed the *Enquirer* and took it to the bathroom where he could read it in private. He did a lot of reading in the bathroom, but this was different. She was pushing him to hurry, knowing that this was going to be very important for her, but not really knowing what it would mean. He was nervous, and she was excited. He knew this feeling well and was really scared, but he wanted to read this as much as she did.

Parts everywhere in the system were scurrying to watch what would happen, and not one of them knew what to say.

Then, voices were everywhere. She was so excited at the possibilities, and he was petrified. His parts were winning each battle
and pushing her further and further down. They had to push
her away and make sure no one knew about her. They could
never let her get control here. One part thought that she would
mutilate them with surgery, and how painful that would be. He
would be the next scandal. There is no way that could happen.
Just no way.

The words, "Don't let her out," came from an entire chorus of his parts. "Deny that she is there," many of them agreed.
"Deny, deny, deny," they said. A few parts volunteered to be
the deniers and agreed they would stay on guard.

She was sad that they were pushing her away, but she
knew that she was true, and now she also was aware that he
knew she was true. That's why he reacted this way. Her best
friend—the Dreamer part told her once again, "It is OK, wait; it
is not your time yet." Once again, sadly, she listened.

Being alone in my apartment allowed her to be out more
and more. The deniers had some time off, as there were no people around to worry about. The few neighbors I had never
knocked on the door, so that concern was low.

She felt like she was growing, getting stronger, and getting a sense of who she may be. Even though she did not ever
leave the apartment, she felt she was not hiding all the time.

He was getting weaker and hiding more. He was getting
even more confused and felt like he was now serving her. He
was not even sure if he had a choice.

There was one thing that was becoming very clearly true
for him. He was getting very, very lonely.

...You Just Might Find, You Get What You Need

No, you can't always get what you want,
But if you try sometime, you just might find,
You get what you need

— "You Can't Always Get What You Want,"
 by Mick Jagger and Keith Richards

Loneliness! There was another part that was so deeply hidden inside of me that so longed to be seen, to be heard, to be connected, and to be reassured that everything would be all right. This part watched all the battling go on for years and had never spoken up as it found one hiding place after another. I knew there was something in there, but never quite knew how to describe it; so many other parts were quick in keeping it hidden.

Only six months had passed since I moved into the apartment, and so much had already happened. The euphoria of being alone, shopping and furnishing, and especially not dealing with the challenges of old relationships had worn off. There was clearly something missing for me, but the ongoing internal struggle clouded any specific idea of what I wanted. I know what she wanted, but that was totally impossible. I wanted to be connected to someone else. I wanted to be in a relationship, but I could not even begin to articulate why. He was pushing me to date—to go out and meet some women. Even though I was fifty-four, the hormones still made them both crazy, and he argued he still had needs!

There were parts that panicked at the thought of dating. I was married for twenty-five years and had kept her a secret.

Now she appeared almost daily. How could I begin a new relationship and keep this secret? It was so clear to me that sharing my secret would prevent any relationship. The old paradox still did not have a solution.

So now there was a new battleground forming between wants and needs. It was becoming hard to understand whether the wants and needs that appeared in me were hers, his, or mine! Needless to say, confusion reigned.

In his classic book *The Four Loves*, C.S. Lewis describes four basic kinds of human love—affection, friendship, erotic love, charity. As I struggled with trying to understand my own wants and needs, it seemed that my hormones still had some drive around the erotic love, but thankfully, now in my mid-fifties, this was diminishing and perhaps being more driven by what I should be feeling rather than how I actually felt. It was becoming more and more clear to me that I needed friendship. One where I could share and be free to be me and not have to hide any of the parts that were within me. At the time, I did not have the words to describe this need for friendship, but I know that it is how I felt. I doubted that it would ever happen. Thankfully it eventually did.

She couldn't wait for the party. She knew she was the only one who would be there, but it really was going to be her first New Year's Eve celebration. Yes, so much happened in 2001, and in a few hours, she would watch the ball drop in Times Square and 2002 would arrive. She bought a new party dress. Her first one really, and could not wait for the evening. She planned on making herself a lovely dinner and even bought some champagne. Just for a sip, of course, as her system never could deal with alcohol.

She knew that he was lonely, and her friends reminded her to reassure him all would be fine, but somehow that never really was a priority for her. She had some trouble relating to his loneliness. After all, he had lived and played and interacted with the world all their life, and she was trapped and hidden. It was really hard for her to relate to his loneliness. She thought about her own loneliness over the past fifty years. She also struggled mightily when his needs—yes, those physical ones (damn hormones) pushed her away.

This was her time to party. At last!

It was shortly after New Year's, and I was chatting with a few people at work about my experience at the *Loving Yourself, Living Fully* seminar that I attended a few months earlier. My co-workers knew I was in process of divorce and moved to my own apartment, and I had great support from them. Little did I know how my life was about to change.

Someone mentioned that I should talk to one of the guys who handled the customer service phones. Apparently this person was also telling people about a great seminar that he went to, and that we should share our experiences with each other. It didn't take me long to go find him. He said that he had just been to a seminar that was run by a group called Insight, and that it was great. He had a huge smile on his face, and when I asked for more details he just kept smiling and told me that I should go, and that I would love it. Honestly, this frustrated me completely as he was steadfast in not providing me any details, yet kept repeating how great it was. For some reason, the name of Insight sounded familiar to me, but I could not quite place it. Later that afternoon, as I racked my brain, I thought I remembered where I heard about it.

When I got home that night, I found the flyer I was handed at the end of the previous workshop I went to. Sure enough it was for the seminar called Insight I: The Awakening Heart, and it showed that the next one was being held in about a week. It was going to be a long seminar. I called the number on the flyer to find out more, and the person answering the phone was pleasant, but he also would not provide specific details. I thought of the omens at work here; I was pointed to the flyer I had ignored before just in time to register for the event. How does this happen? After the recent crisis I went through, the new me was starting to believe in the crazy connections like this. I don't really understand why, perhaps out of desperation, perhaps out of a willingness to try anything now, but I registered over the phone. I was not sure what I was getting myself into, but if I could get the same smile I saw on my co-worker's face, it would be worth it. Spoiler alert: it was!

From a Wednesday evening through the following Monday evening with all day Friday through Sunday I spent over fifty hours in this seminar. It was like nothing I have ever done before and even with my protector parts that were on guard for most of the time. They were so on guard! There was even an exercise where they totally shut me down from participating. However, that exact act did more to impact me than all the other work done at the seminar. The exercise took place late on Sunday morning, and I spent the rest of the afternoon trying to understand why I froze. Many participants wanted to check in on me, and I was like a statue, and then started to cry. I managed to come back to some form of consciousness after lunch, and a few hours later realized that I needed more of whatever was happening and some connection to the people in that room over the weekend. Then I did something that I had never done before. When they asked if anyone was willing to volunteer to help make phone calls to invite people to the next seminar, I raised my hand. All my hiding parts were aghast when my arm went up. They could not imagine that I would join or volunteer for anything. They all were worried.

The Awakening Heart seminar still occurs and focuses on topics that include personal responsibility, choice, the power of commitment and intention, forgiveness, and authenticity. Many of these characteristics I sorely lacked. Perhaps that is why I felt like I could not leave the room. Certainly the concept of authenticity for me, especially in a public forum, was painfully challenging. Over the next eighteen months, I was involved with one seminar or another every month as either an attendee or as a volunteer assistant. I also met a young woman who has become my best friend.

I Saw Her Standing There

We had weekly meetings where we got to chat and check in about how we were doing. Then we made cold calls to names on an interest list to see if people were interested in either attending the next seminar or coming to an introduction. I was interacting with people, both men and women as friends with a common purpose. I had never done this before. Although I had parts on guard, I loved this time. We started in early February 2002, and we knew there was going to be another seminar in July and an introductory evening session in June. I also volunteered to be an assistant at the July seminar. All of this was so new for me.

I agreed to help out at the intro evening and got to the hotel early to help set up the room. Just like the seminar, the intro is a small mixture of lecture and experiential exercises so people can talk and interact, and they get a sense of what the format is. It usually works quite well, and many people choose to attend the seminar after experiencing the introduction.

He was aware that it was almost a year since he was no longer part of a couple. So much had already happened, a great deal of which he felt he had no control over. She was so present now, but he really felt lonely, and it was wearing on him greatly. He never was really good at dating even in the old days, but felt he had to meet someone. How could he do this and still keep his secret? "Lie if you have to," kept flowing through his mind.

There was a woman I met at the January seminar that I asked to dinner. Thinking back to this, as a first date after a long-term marriage, I spent most of the dinner being a victim of my situation and talking about my divorce. I was clueless and had no idea what I was doing. I cannot even imagine what this woman was thinking of me. Afterwards, I felt like a fool and embarrassed for days.

In the spring of 2002, I put an ad in one of the online dating boards. I was: DWM 54 (fifty-four year old, divorced white male) looking for friendship. I was clearly not asking for an LTR (long term relationship) that it seemed like every woman on the boards had in their ads. I met one woman on the dating board and got past a first date. I asked if she would like to go kayaking on a second date, and she agreed. She came wearing heels. This did not work out well. Her ad stated she was a nonsmoker, but she needed breaks to smoke. Perhaps I was not the only one with secrets to hide.

There was a good crowd at the seminar intro meeting. A young woman introduced herself as Tessa. Gosh she was young, in her twenties, I thought. There was something about her though, that I could not stop watching her.

A month later, I was assisting at the seminar and Tessa was a very active participant in it. I had parts that were captivated by her and her story. Many of the group of people at this seminar became friends and started to have some get-togethers. I got to meet Tessa at a party and then a picnic later in the summer and had some conversations with her. I was getting that "can't get her out of my mind" feeling that I knew was totally impossible and made no sense.

In October 2002, we were both participants in a seminar, and we had a chance to work together in a few experiential exercises. After the last evening of the seminar, a group of people went out to grab a late bite. I offered to drive Tessa and a few other people. When we were done, we chatted in my car for a bit, and well, somehow a great friendship began. I learned that relationships are also like snowflakes in that no two are the same. I also learned to both be and have a friend.

We both still look back on this moment, and neither of us understands how we created the friendship we have, as at first, I ignored all the reasons for NO! and later, we both evolved and changed so much. We often joke that we do not have any words to describe why or how our friendship works, it just does. Since we don't understand it ourselves, it is hard to explain to others.

I still am not certain that at that time I knew what I wanted. But I did know that I needed a friend, a best friend. I never really had one before.

As it turned out, thankfully, I got what I needed!

First Confession

Vulnerability is about showing up and being seen. It's tough to do that when we're terrified about what people might see or think.

—Brené Brown

At about the same time Tessa and I started to hang out together, I was laid off from my job as a director of program management. It was the fall of 2002 and the end of the period of irrational exuberance in the tech world. I had some severance and I could survive on unemployment for a year. I had plenty of time on my hands as I looked, pretty hopelessly, for a job. I spent a good deal of time with Tessa.

She wasn't sure how she felt about this new person, Tessa, in his life. It was hard for *her* because there were times she wanted to be out and dressed and once again had to fight for her time and space. She knew that he was happier than he had been in a long time, but she was not going to give in to his needs that easily. She was not going back into hiding. She knew what she wanted and realized that she, once again, would have to fight for it!

I had no idea how to be in a new friendship. Tessa and I talked and shared so much together. In many ways, I was vulnerable—although not about the gender war that was inside me. We took turns talking and listening and just being there for each other. Neither of us understood why; with the vast differences in our backgrounds, we were able to communicate and felt comfortable, and respectful with each other. For both of us it was a new experience of friendship that both of us had lacked.

I was really struggling. In some sense, I was baring my soul to Tessa, yet I was hiding what was inside of me. I knew that I did not want to begin a new relationship and hide again. I didn't even know what a friendship or relationship could be. That damn isolation paradox was rising up once again, and the chatter in my head would not stop. I had to decide what to do. I was coming up to a crossroad and had to choose a path to go down.

He was so afraid that if Tessa found out, not only would the friendship be over, but also it was likely there would never be a chance for any future friendships.

She just wanted to get it over with and figured that it would be over and she would have more time to run the system. That's all she really cared about. She was pretty upset that she did not get to have another New Year's party by herself. Tessa came over and *they* were having dinner. *She* was losing control!

They both had their friends and allies in the system. The noise was nonstop!

As January ended, it was getting harder and harder for me to deal with the dilemma. I knew I would have to share with Tessa, and I also knew that it would end the relationship. But I could hide no longer. It was in early February 2003 when I was at Tessa's apartment and not in a good space. I was crying and finally broke down, and she wanted to know what was bothering me.

"I wear women's clothes. I am a cross-dresser," came out between the tears.

"Whatever floats your boat," she calmly responded and hugged me.

I looked at her in astonishment as I tried to catch my breath. I was not shamed nor banished. She did not seem to be phased by my confession, and I truly did not understand what just happened or what it would mean. I had expected a shocking response, but not this type of shock. Tessa is the first person I ever shared my innermost secret with. I was not rejected out of hand. I really was not prepared for this outcome.

We talked some more about the situation, and she said that it didn't bother her, but that it was not something that she wanted to be part of. She was OK talking about it, and even seeing pictures, but she did not have any interest in seeing me dressed up. This was more than I ever expected. Our friendship did not end, and over time I found, although with some difficulty, I could separate my time for Tessa and for the girl inside of me.

They were both shocked. Yet they both thought that each of them had really found a friend.

He was not abandoned, and it seemed that he had a friend.

She thought that somebody now knows she exists. She never, ever believed this would happen. Even if Tessa only got to see her pictures, that would be amazing, just amazing. She was not sure if this would be worth backing off on control and giving him some more space, but she was willing to see what might happen.

I was tentative in sharing some pictures with Tessa and really did not want to have this overwhelm our relationship. I learned to separate these parts of my life in some manner. I seemed to have a few separate lives going on now: a job-hunting life, a life with my kids, time with Tessa, and a life with her. I was learning how to find a balance, as I thought how lucky I was.

Tessa once asked me if the girl part of me had a name. I always wrestled with this question and never was able to select one. Tessa made a suggestion. At the seminars we attended there was a concept that when one's life is going well it is operating with "ease and grace." Tessa suggested that Tessa would be "Ease" and the girl in me would be "Grace." I was stunned as I took this name in. I thought the name Grace carried so many other meanings with it. How could that be me? I loved it immediately but thought that it was more of a wish of who I wanted to be rather than who I was. I had previously thought that if I ever changed my name, I would use my middle name as the root of a new surname. So I tried on the sound of Grace Stevens. Tessa suggested that I add her own middle name of Anne.

It was like breaking a bottle of champagne on the hull of a boat at its launching. Grace Anne Stevens was named! At the time, I had no idea that I would eventually transition and legally change my name to this. No idea at all.

After I transitioned and shared this news with some colleagues via social media, one response that always makes me laugh was, "Oh you transitioned from being Jewish to Irish Catholic, cool!"

Transgender people have the opportunity to rename themselves. Many will give themselves a new first name, and there are a few, like me, who change all their names including their surname. I suspect each of us has our own reasons for doing what they do. I know many people who try on many names before they find just the right one, whether they transition or not.

I believe that names can be empowering to the hidden parts inside of us. I have taken part in naming ceremonies and am aware of some religious organizations that are creating naming ceremonies for transgender people who transition. This is such a wonderful sign of acceptance and understanding of our experience.

For me the formal saying and claiming of my name, my identity, in a public forum was incredibly powerful. For anyone who, for whatever reason, may change his or her name, I suggest that you take part in such a ceremony, even if you create it yourself.

I asked my kids once if they were upset that I no longer had the same surname as they did. I hope they were honest when they said they were not concerned.

Many people ask me how I chose my name. I share this story and tell them that I did not choose it. The name was a gift from Tessa, the first person I confessed my truth to. It is a gift that I will always treasure.

Reinventions

Every moment is a fork in the road.
The road you take will shape your future.
Choose love over fear.

—unknown source

I graduated college in 1969 with a bachelor's degree in engineering and received a handful of job offers in different areas of the country. I truly thought that my future was assured. I had no idea what the world of working was like.

I mentioned earlier that throughout my engineering career, I found myself unemployed, and not by my choice, in each decade. This happened in 1971, 1986, 1993, 2002, and 2013. Each time was scary.

In 1971, I was young and single and was out of work for almost eighteen months. My first job was focused on military work, and at the end of the war in Vietnam, the government money disappeared. After a year of unemployment, I took an hourly job in a retail store for minimum wage. I applied and was accepted for a master's degree program in engineering at Penn State but found a new engineering job a few months before I had to go. At this fork in the road, I chose to stay working, and it was where I really learned how to be an engineer. I learned how to design computers that controlled missile guidance systems. This job lasted seven years before I chose to move on. During this time, I got married and started a family. I became a husband, a father, perhaps even an adult. I was still hiding what was inside me.

The late seventies and early eighties were the time of startup companies where the dream of stock and money was prevalent throughout the engineering community. Entrepreneurs and venture capitalists seemed like they were everywhere. Yes, you would have to put in many hours, but the hope of striking it rich was out there. However, I learned the hard way that many of these startup companies do not succeed, and there is always the risk of losing your job.

This happened to me in 1986 and again in 1993. Luckily, both times it took me only three to four months to find another position. It was scary, but each time it worked out fine. It was different in 2002. I was fifty-four years old, and a senior engineering manager. The dot-com bubble had just burst. There were no jobs. At that point I was living alone. Luckily at my last job change in 2000, I ended up selling some stock from the company I was at while the irrational market was still high. I had many co-workers who held the stock and eventually lost any potential gains they saw on paper. I was out of work but I was debt free. Again, I consider myself lucky.

As far as finding a job, I had no idea what to do, and once again, I was very scared. My gender issues were starting to take over me. I had just found a new friend, and I had no idea if I would ever find a job again. I wanted to believe it would all work out, but I was still scared of the unknown.

My spirits were low as I did not receive a single response to any resumes I sent out. After a year, my unemployment benefits had run out, and I was confused and a bit desperate. It was the fall of 2003. I walked into the Sears in the local mall and asked for a job. I was immediately hired by the HR person to sell refrigerators. This job had no salary and was 100 percent commission. This was an interesting experience. In some sense, each shift was survival of the fittest. The salespeople would trip over each other to greet customers approaching the floor, do a quick assessment of whether they are a looker or a buyer, and then push forward to introduce themselves first as their salesperson.

I was aware I had a part that thought that by getting in front of the public and learning how to sell would give me a great new skill that perhaps someday would lead to something greater. My arrogant Know-It-All part thought that convincing people to buy something couldn't be that hard. They both turned out to be very wrong. There were a few nice people that I worked with who were willing to share their experience and knowledge with me, and there were a few who, let me just say, were less than trustworthy. This was a very different world, or perhaps I should say universe, that I was not familiar with. I felt very out of place there. For me it was a form of survival. It made me think what it was like for my parents growing up during the great depression, and how much I still had to be thankful for. It was not easy, and I still struggled with what to do. I kept sending out resumes and reading reports that the tech market was getting better, but I had no direct proof. Nine months of selling refrigerators passed, and I was barely making enough to survive and was depleting most of my savings. I had to do something else.

I continued to call and meet with people I knew to network, and a few made the suggestion that I should get certified as a program manager, which might provide more opportunity for jobs. I had previously held senior engineering positions that included a one-year position as a vice president of engineering and numerous director level jobs. I not only could build and lead teams, but I brought up and debugged manufacturing lines both in the U.S. and in Asia. I had a great deal of experience that no longer seemed to be in demand. I wrestled with the idea of signing up for a short course to train for the PMP (Project Management Professional) exam. It cost about $2,500 and my funds were low.

I wrestled about this idea for weeks. I still had received no responses from any resumes I sent out. I had been out of the tech world for eighteen months already. I remembered from all the seminars I attended one of the lessons taught: the universe rewards action.

It was late September 2004 as I started to apply for program management jobs, and I sent a check to register for the course. Apparently the universe did reward action. Within the next few weeks, I received responses from five different companies to come for an interview. Over the next few weeks, I interviewed at these companies and a few had me back for a second interview. Luckily, one turned into a job offer. I was reinvented as a program manager and back in the tech world. I was rescued. I was saved. It was just in time, as I was not certain how I would pay my rent the next month.

I started work the Monday of Thanksgiving week 2004. For two years, I had been out of the tech world and was now back in it. I was lucky. I had a job. At fifty-seven years old, I worried about how long this job would last. What would I do next? While very good at leading teams in technical development projects, I was very bad at selling refrigerators. I really had no individual portable skill. But now, money was coming in, and these thoughts were fading into the background.

She spent a lot of time out during the days at home, and she worried. As soon as I received the job offer, she went crazy ordering new clothes and also grabbed some things off the floor at Sears before they lost the employee discount. She did have her priorities.

At the first Insight seminar I attended, we were randomly assigned buddies. They suggested that we meet after the seminar. My buddy was a woman whom I met with after the seminar to go skiing, and we made it an annual event. We did run into each other at some other seminars, but we mostly caught up as we rode on the lifts for a day of skiing.

There were a number of people from the seminars who were very vocal about wanting to become seminar facilitators. They wanted to be on stage in front of 50 to 100 people and teach and process what they felt, and to help people change their lives. I had similar but not exactly the same feelings. I had parts watching the facilitators and trying to understand what they were doing. At the same time, I had parts guarding closely to ensure my secrets didn't leak out, and then there were parts that were willing to take in and try to assimilate the new information into my system. I did have a part that wanted to be a facilitator, but I had more parts that were clear that I could not do that until I had the skills of a facilitator. I wanted those skills—whatever they were. A seed was planted in my mind. This combined with

my ongoing journey of trying to understand my own gender issues, and I started to think whether I should go back to school to
get a degree in psychology. At the time, it was a dream with no
plan or reality associated with it.

I had shared these thoughts on a ski lift with my buddy in
2003 and 2004. When I brought it up once again in early 2005,
she stared at me and quite starkly called me out. She said I was
full of shit. She did not believe I would ever do it and advised
me to stop talking about it. I was duly embarrassed and wondered what was stopping me. Was it the money, the commitment, or that perhaps I really did not want to find my truth?

I was working and had few responsibilities. Perhaps I
could gain a new individual portable skill. Tessa was already
back in school to get a master's in acupuncture. I had the time.
Within a month I applied to a program that could lead to a master's in counseling psychology. It would take four years going to
school two to three nights a week including summers, and
somehow I would have to figure out how to do an internship.
The idea was nuts. I had no idea if I would ever complete it.

I was invited for an interview and asked why I wanted to
get a degree in counseling. My old Know-It-All part jumped
right in. "I am an engineer and a program manager, and I am
going to fix people," came right out. The interviewer gave me a
knowing smile and nodded her head. At the time, I did not
know why.

I was accepted and went back to school in September
2005. After orientation and one course, I understood that knowing smile. Counselors do not fix anyone or anything. Individuals
are all responsible for helping themselves. Sometimes people
need some guidance, some coaching, and some support to help

them. I am still learning this for myself and for people I work with.

Beginning of the End or End of the Beginning?

Often when you think you're at the end of something, you're at the beginning of something else.

—Fred Rogers

2007 was a pretty big milestone year. I would be turning sixty. The kids were all out of college now and chasing their own dreams. Simi and Elie were both married. Three years earlier, Simi had a plan. He asked me if I could stay in shape for at least three more years, and when I turn sixty, we could do another road trip. This time we could go to Moab and go mountain biking. When I turned fifty, I started to bike again after not doing this for over twenty-five years. I dreamt about going to Moab and would often talk about it like this: "Maybe, someday, I would love to bike in Moab." I don't think I would have ever thought of doing this on my own, but when Simi put the idea out, I jumped at it. The trip was planned before the boys got married, three years in the planning. Stella was originally going to join us, too, but she ended up on a conflicting trip. In May 2007, we took the road trip, which we called Mo '07. We even had T-shirts made with a logo for the trip. I took the boys away from their wives for ten days. I am sure this will not happen again. Elie lived in Tucson and Simi and I flew into Phoenix. Elie picked us up, and we drove north. It was a long day, and we stopped in Flagstaff before continuing on to Moab, Arches National Park, and Canyonlands National Park, then back through the Grand Canyon and Sedona before returning to Tucson. We backcountry camped and rented bikes and had an awesome time. Mo '07 was a huge success.

All throughout the trip, I was struggling with turning sixty and what to do about her.

She was struggling. Just getting dressed and sitting around was not enough for her anymore. She wanted more but didn't know what more meant. She was getting old. Tessa once looked at a picture and said she looked like a "beautiful, ugly old Jewish woman," and said it was a compliment. All she heard was "ugly" and "old." It sure did not sound like a compliment.

She wanted to get out. She wanted to be in the world. He would never let her. She kept fighting to get out.

We climbed Cathedral Rock when we were in Sedona, Arizona. It was our last stop before we drove back to Tucson, and I would return the boys to their wives. Cathedral Rock is

Climbing Cathedral Rock.

rumored to have vortexes of channeled energy, and climbing to these vortexes is the goal of many hikers. I remember sitting on the edge of an outlook as we climbed. I was looking for a vortex—a form of energy that would guide me to my future. The boys made fun of me—once again. Perhaps I did receive the guidance I sought. However I did not know it then.

She reluctantly agreed that the trip was great but now that she was home she wanted to go out. She did not want to be either ugly or old, which so stuck with her, and she was in fear of turning sixty. She wanted to go out and get a makeover—a glam makeover—and get pictures of how pretty she could be. She was ready and would not take no for an answer.

I was petrified driving out for the makeover. I called it my birthday present to myself. I reserved a full day makeover with someone

Glam photo.

who was well known on the Internet. I had a huge duffel bag full of clothes, even though I knew I did not need them.

The day was crazy. She was strapped into a corset and could not breathe if she sat down, which was barely possible. She wore flesh colored tights covered with pantyhose. There was padding where appropriate; her face was taped for an instant face-lift, and then on top, layers and layers of makeup. Wigs were also layered on her head. Over a five- to six-hour period and through three changes of outfits, I took hundreds of pictures. A few were more risqué than I thought I would ever take, but the experience was mind-blowing—so many pictures. She was very happy.

On the drive home, I did not know what to think. I just went to my own fantasyland. I knew it was not real and did not represent any form of reality. But the experience had planted the seed of possibility. *Maybe, just maybe.*

I completed my second year of counseling psychology classes during the summer and realized that I would be able to complete all the required classes within the next year. I still was not sure if I would be able to figure out how to do the internship requirement the following year, but I was moving forward without knowing. I was planning which course I would take in both the fall and the spring semesters.

There was a class being offered in the spring semester titled Counseling LGBT Clients. I knew I had to take it, but I had an entire chorus of parts warning me that if I did, my secret would come out. I had parts that wanted this to happen and parts that didn't. If I could not come out in a counseling class, where in the world could I ever come out?

Tessa kept telling me that she knew I would take the class. I was not so certain. My anxiety level was through the roof. Late in the fall of 2007 I had to make the decision. I signed up for the class, which began in January 2008. There were thirteen people in the class during the first session. I had been in class with some of them before. There was only one other guy in the class. The instructor asked us to introduce ourselves and say what our interest in taking this class was. I knew this question was coming. I was prepared to be truthful, but perhaps not fully—yet. When it was my turn, I not-so-calmly said, "I have been struggling with gender issues all my life." I expected the world to collapse on top of me. I expected everyone would look and point and want to know more. This didn't happen, and the next person went. The class went on and no one talked to me about it.

So far, so good, I thought. I knew it wasn't time yet, I knew the syllabus required a project with a presentation. I knew I would be doing a project on Male to Female Transgender, and that I would be coming out as part of the presentation. I knew that I had to. It was a plan, it was going to happen, and I was still a wreck up until the moment I was in front of the room.

YES!

The Elephant in the Room

Come out, come out wherever you are
And meet the young lady who fell from a star
She fell from the sky, she fell very far
And Kansas she says is the name of the star

—Glinda, in *The Wizard of OZ*

I put so much work into the presentation. There was no way that I would be able to do it in the fifteen minutes, the allotted time. My own dry runs took at least twice that. I did not even worry about the limitation, as this entire event was taking on a life of its own. I had a title slide that called the presentation *Under the Transgender Umbrella: Male to Female,* and had an umbrella animated as it slid into the middle of the slide. I also had music embedded in the presentation, and the Who's "*Who Are You?*" was playing in the background.

I would come out to the class at the start and then proceed to teach them about Male to Female trans people. Mind you, at this time, all my knowledge was from books and the Internet, and the single interview I did with someone I knew. Except for Tessa, I was still extremely and totally closeted.

She was ready. It was like standing on the edge of a knife and balancing precariously. How could she be so anxious and so calm at the same time? She had no idea what would happen, but she needed to take another step in no longer hiding, even if it was a small one.

I started with a cartoon from *The Far Side* and had it fade in. It showed a couple searching their bedroom with an elephant crouching down and hiding behind a dresser, which had all the drawers open, and the clothes scattered around. The husband and wife are searching for something and the caption is, "Now calm down, Barbara. We haven't looked everywhere yet, and an elephant can't hide in here forever."

As it faded in, I announced that I am doing this presentation about male to female transgender because I am transgender.

I named it; I claimed it. I identified myself to my classmates, many who were strangers to me, as being transgender. I was so hoping that by choosing this fork in the road I was choosing love over fear. I know I asked for confidentiality in what I was sharing, and I knew there was risk in what I was doing, and well, you know how it usually goes.

The room went silent. Everyone was now totally focused on me. I had their 100 percent attention. I took a deep breath and continued. I taught about so many topics; how transgender people feel, their fears, what they may do to express their truth, and types of surgeries that people may opt for. I shared stories, pictures, and videos that showed personal experiences.

I then shared my own story and told them that except for Tessa, this was my coming out experience. I shared pictures from the Big Closet days and also from the glam makeover. When they saw the photos, they were astonished—as I have been—since I cannot recognize myself in them. It took me forty-five minutes to get through the entire presentation. I have some trouble remembering what happened after my classmates and the instructor stood up and applauded me. I don't know if it was only one or a group of my parts that took me somewhere else. I think I heard one say, "OK, you dropped the damn grenade; now let's get the hell out of here!"

I know the class broke for lunch. I am a complete blank after that.

She was still balancing on the edge and had no idea what to do next. Should she talk, or wait until someone talks to her? She saw him in the background bending over and hitting his legs with his fist and noticed he was crying. She did not know why and really could not focus on him. She was not totally hidden anymore. She really hoped it would be OK. She really did.

After lunch, I had to meet with the teacher to get feedback on my presentation. I did not know what to expect. She shared that she was astounded in that she had never seen anyone combine a coming out with an in-depth teaching experience and was totally amazed by what I had done. I had a hard time keeping my know-it-all and arrogant parts from jumping up and down, but this feedback felt great. I learned an important lesson that I did not make good use of until a few years later. I learned that when I am open and honest, when I am vulnerable to let people see my truth, it provides a teaching experience that is hard to match. Letting the elephant in the room out and being seen made a difference not only to me, but to the people I shared it with.

The deed was done, and I had no idea if more people knew. I started to selectively share with people. I would often meet up with different people in the cafeteria to chat. I shared with one of my classmates, and she told me she already knew but was not going to mention it until I did. There was a small circle of people that I was comfortable talking about this part of me with. The spring semester ended, and I was hoping that I did the right thing. Grace still never went out of the house. This was still too scary.

By the fall semester, I had already found some community, and one day before class, one of the girls said she always liked going to shows but had no one to go with.

In a blink of an eye, *she* grabbed control and asked my classmate if she would be willing to go to a show with Grace? "Of course, yes," was the response and another classmate also jumped in and asked to go, and another said she would love to join us.

Grace seemed to now have girlfriends. Real girls, real girlfriends. We were all counseling students, and the others were fine being out with Grace. Could it get any better?

For the next few years we got together every few months to go out. This was so life-changing for me. One of my friends came with me the first time I went to buy a wig in person to help me pick it out. Another friend invited me to her wedding in

2013. I had not seen her in a few years, but I was so excited to go.

Choosing love over fear was the right thing to do. I was blessed.

Community

A community is like a ship;
Everyone ought to be prepared to take the helm.

—Henrik Ibsen

The presentation at school took place in March 2008. It was a great and positive step. I learned I could say the words "I" and "transgender" in the same sentence. However, it was not enough. She was clamoring to get out—to BE out.

For the past few years I had been following so many people and groups on the Internet, I was aware that there was a support group in the next town. I was aware that they had weekly meetings, and their website had the theme "You are not alone." Certainly I felt alone. I felt alone for over sixty years. The group was called The Tiffany Club of New England and had a long history. It started out as a club for cross-dressers where they could meet and dress in privacy without having to rent a hotel room.

My own Big Closet was not enough anymore. That was clear. What to do about it was not so clear. It was a Tuesday night in May 2008, and I called the phone number. It rang and someone picked up, and I heard, "Hello, Tiffany Club."

I froze. My hand was shaking and the rest of my body soon joined it. I had no idea what to say, or what I wanted. I hung up the phone.

One week later I called again.

"Hello, Tiffany Club, this is Janet!"

This time I responded and said hello. Words stumbled out of my mouth in an unorganized manner.

"Uh, I want to know something about the club," I asked.

"Why would you like to know?"

"Uh, well, I am a cross-dresser."

"Ok, that's great, many of us here are, and you would be welcome to come and meet us. You can come dressed or there are changing rooms here if you would like."

"Thanks so much, can I come next week?"

"That would be great. I look forward to meeting you."

OMG. What had I just done? What kinds of people were at that place? Do they have sex there? Do they drink there? That's not what I wanted. What was I going to do?

The next Tuesday I drove over to the club. I had a bag of clothes with me, hoping that I would be able to change. My heart was beating so fast I thought it would explode out of my chest. I found the door on the street and climbed the staircase. I put my hand on the doorknob, and it seemed like it took me an hour before I could turn it and walk in. The room was full with people. Some were in women's clothes, and some were in men's. There were a few rooms with people all around. I was invited to sit down, and people introduced themselves. There were some couples there. There were some people I was unclear as to what gender they might be. I walked across another threshold.

Everyone was very nice, yet I had so many parts in a precarious balance of being on guard, wanting to run out of there,
and wanting to spill my guts out to everyone. People wanted to
talk, and I wondered if I would ever get a chance to change my
clothes. I thought I was prepared, but then someone asked me a
question that I apparently was not able to answer. I learned that
this was *the* question that almost every person would ask someone when they first meet them at the club, and I also eventually
learned why.

"How do you identify?"

"Uh...what do you mean?" I responded a bit confused.

"Are you CD or TS?"

She wanted to jump out and yell at the top of her lungs
that of course she is a girl. He, and his inner friends, though a bit
confused, were able to hold her back from taking control. Even
her friends were helping out with this. Not now, too soon, they
reminded her.

He tried to process the question. CD means cross-dresser
and TS means transsexual. He knew the words and what they
meant. He could never say the word transsexual out loud. He
was so afraid that if he said it, if he gave it life by saying it out
loud, it would make it true. He wasn't there yet.

She was, and always had been.

"I don't really know, I am trying to figure it all out," was
my feeble response.

People around the table nodded as if they had heard this
all before and seemed to get quiet. Laura invited me into the office to interview me in more detail. They wanted to be sure I was

really a fit. To begin with they wanted to make sure that I really was transgender and not what is called an admirer. At this time I had no idea what this meant. I learned that admirers are men who are interested in transgender girls for what may often be, but not necessarily, sexual encounters. Well, here were some more "snowflakes" with another unique set of desires and behaviors. I was getting quite an education here. I learned that the club had a long and interesting history. The rules of the club now included no alcohol, drugs, or sex. This was not a dating club; it was a support group for gender variant people. This was a great relief. The talking went on and on, so I eventually just asked if it would be OK if I could change my clothes.

Grace made her first appearance in front of other people that night. As I mingled around and introduced myself, each one of them continued to ask me the question, "How do you identify?"

I learned why they ask. The Tiffany Club was officially incorporated as a nonprofit charitable organization in 1989 to provide support for the transgender community. It had been around earlier than 1989 as a safe place for cross-dressers to come and be with others like themselves, before it was safe to go out on their own. There were many women who had passed through the club and eventually realized that they were not just cross-dressers, but transsexual and proceeded to transition. Upon transition, the vast majority chose to leave the club and any friends they had made, and go on to live their lives in their new gender, while cutting ties to their past. I learned that many of the people at the club, felt burned by these experiences, and that when new people came to the club, if they would identify as TS, the old-timers, the cross-dressers at the club may not want to invest in a new relationship, as they feared it would eventually be abandoned. By not stating an identity, I was given a little space to chat with everyone.

I chatted with a lot of people that night. I had brought a skirt and top and makeup. I had no idea how I looked, but it felt great. The club has a theme that states, "You are not alone." They were right; I was not alone. I was chatting with a tall blond cross-dresser who looked great. It was getting late and almost time to go home. I said that I wished I could go home dressed like this. She looked at me and asked, "Why can't you?"

Uh oh. There was a fork in the road. The maybe path was blocked; I had to choose between the yes or the no path.

It was 11:00 p.m. It was dark out. I went home cross-dressed. I was in panic at each red light, when a car stopped in the lane next to me. I kept my eyes locked straight ahead. I didn't want to see if anyone was looking at me.

I lived in an apartment on the second floor of a condo complex. As I pulled into my parking space, I wondered if I could make it across the parking lot, and up the stairs unnoticed. I worried that someone would be looking out their windows. Just a bit of paranoia.

I made it upstairs and fumbled with the keys in the lock. I was in my apartment, safe. I couldn't sit down. It took a long time for my heart to slow down. Same for my brain. My life had just changed.

Four days later, on Saturday night there was a house party at the club. It was 7:00 p.m. and still light out. Grace was dressed and ready to go out. I opened my apartment door and peeked out. It was all clear. I ran down the hallway and looked out the window that overlooked the parking lot. There were a few kids playing on the grass. Could I make it? I waited, waited, and then went for it. I must have held my breath for minutes as my chest was pounding. I cleared the parking lot and could take a breath. I learned how to avoid aligning with cars next to me at red lights.

Grace went out like this each Tuesday night, and every other Saturday when the club was open. Each time it felt as if my heart was in my throat. I was petrified but did it anyway! It did not feel easy for a long time. About a year later, I sent a letter to my neighbors telling them I was transgender, and it became easier coming and going. As I occasionally ran into them, each was cool and had varied levels of interest and experience—even the little kids, although they got confused about what name to call me. There was a four-year-old girl who saw me leaving one evening, and as I got in my car I heard her ask her mom, "Why is that man wearing a skirt?" As I drove off, I was watching her mom try to explain.

There was also a boy who was about six or seven years old who would always say hello to me. One day as Grace was leaving, he said, "Hi Larnie, oh, I mean Grace, oh...whatever!"

It took me a few months before I let some of the women at the club convince me to go out to a restaurant and bar with them on a Saturday night. I knew the panic feeling well by then and overcame it. Another step forward and I eventually became comfortable enough to take out women that came to the club after me.

We chatted, and I heard more of the history of the club and the politics. Oh my, I had no idea about the diversity and the personalities. All the years hiding from groups and people left me surprised what goes on in groups. I learned much, and I learned quickly. I learned that the club was in a financial mess, and the present leadership was in the process of leaving. Within a year of first going out, I found myself in a leadership position of a transgender support group. My Take-Charge part jumped right in, without a clue as to where it would lead.

My First Event

As I became a regular attendee and member of The Tiffany Club, I kept hearing mention of "First Event," the annual conference held each January. I learned that the conference was organized and run by the club and was the primary fundraiser that helped pay the rent and utilities for the club. Tiffany Club may be the only transgender support group that has a brick and mortar facility where members can come on their own schedule.

Members told me I must go to the conference. There would be hundreds of people there and many workshops for education. Oh, and then there would be dancing in the evening. I made my plans to attend.

It was January 2009. It had been about nine months since the day I first went to The Tiffany Club. I had been out a few times to restaurants with the other women. I was becoming comfortable presenting female, as Grace Stevens, although my heart still beat faster than normal when I was out. I even made up a business card with my picture on it, if there was an opportunity to meet others. I hoped they would remember me. I brought no male clothes. I was about to live as Grace 24/7 for four days.

I never had an idea what this experience would do to me. I entered what seemed like a fantasyland. I fell into a fairy tale.

A few years later, for the program guide of First Event 2013, I wrote about this experience. Here is some of it.

Fairy Tales

Growing up in the fifties and sixties, along with knowing and hiding that I am not a boy was, as many of you well understand, a challenge. My drug of choice to escape was my family's Dumont TV that was more or less my parent. Sitting in front of it for many hours each day is where I learned about the world. Even though there was not the almost infinite choice of cable channels that are available today, the content was more than sufficient.

Every Saturday and Sunday morning I watched movies of one fairy tale after another, and I was glued to them. Magic and sorcery and dreams coming true and living happily after. What better escape for a young, hidden trans child?

Good always triumphed over evil, so the heroine was saved to live happily ever after. I would dream about when and how I would be saved. Perhaps I was just never good enough. Drat!

Like Sleeping Beauty, I lived my life for decades not being fully awake and engaged with the world around me.

Like Oz the Great and Powerful, I hid behind a curtain and manipulated the people in my life without having any real power.

If you are from my generation, you may remember those great live broadcasts of *Peter Pan*. I remember when Tinker Bell is dying and Peter asks all of us watching to believe, to truly believe in fairies, which is the only way to save her. Of course I joined in, and Tinker Bell was saved, but I always wondered who will believe in me and when will I be saved? Who could or would love me and save me from the monsters within me? Would I ever have my dreams come true and live happily ever after?

The years turned into decades. I married and raised three awesome kids. I continued to hide and to dream, but it became harder and harder to find a way to escape.

Then through a variety of circumstances and situations I knew I could hide no longer and made the scariest decision of my life up to that time and dared to visit The Tiffany Club of New England in May 2008. I survived that first visit and through the summer I was told I must go to First Event. In January 2009, I made my first voyage through the Looking Glass and attended First Event. Yes, I was the woman whose jaw was dropping to the floor everywhere I turned. There were hundreds of people like me. Most were having the grandest of times. I met women that had transitioned, and oh my, some who even had surgery! They seemed normal and happy. I attended workshops, and my head was spinning. There was magic and sorcery. Nothing was impossible. An old guy could change his face, his voice, his hair, his skin, his chest, and his genitals. Everything is possible, and there were girls that showed it and were more than willing to share their experience and journeys.

At First Event 2009, I learned that dreams can and do come true. Now I had to figure out what my dream really was since nothing was impossible anymore.

Nothing was impossible and dreams come true!

I left First Event on Sunday afternoon in a daze. When I got home, I sat on my couch for hours. I could not change back into male clothes until the next morning when I went to work. What would I ever do now?

I met a gender therapist at First Event that many people recommended. I made an appointment with her. I had no idea what I wanted. Or at least that was what He kept telling me. She had another opinion.

When I first met the therapist, she mentioned that for most cross-dressers, when they return from a conference, they feel great and are ready to get right back into their male persona. For those who are transsexual, she said, they might have a difficult time returning into their everyday male mode.

I was so good at denial.

After completing my internship at a substance abuse clinic, I graduated with an MA in Counseling Psychology in May 2009. I continued to work a few nights a week in the clinic, gaining a new individual portable skill, while still working by day as a program manager in the tech world. I was working in dual careers having earned two degrees forty years apart. Amazing!

At the clinic, I started to facilitate psycho-education classes for first offender drunk drivers. This is a sixteen week (forty hours) mandated program after an initial OUI violation.

Getting an OUI did not mean a person was an alcoholic or had a dependency on alcohol. Perhaps they were, perhaps they just drank too much that one time, or perhaps they drove many times without regard that they were affected by the drugs and alcohol. During the course, there were two topics that I taught that had a different personal meaning to me. These were denial and stages of change.

For people with addictions or dependencies, breaking through the many forms of denial is important to realize that they may have a problem that needs to be dealt with. Stages of change is a defined process that has been found to be helpful in addiction clinics where people learn that nothing can change until they first recognize a problem. Then they must make a determination, create a plan, take and maintain action. Relapse may well occur and the path starts over again.

On the evenings that I taught these topics, I would go home and once again cry on my couch. It was so hard to say the word, the sentence, and to own it, but I knew it was true!

I am transsexual.

I had so many parts that would help in denying this. They worked so hard for so long. If I ever stopped denying this, then what would I do next? I know that people transition. I have met some of them. Would I, could I ever have surgery? The idea was so scary.

I was at the stage where I now accepted the problem. The next stage was defined as the planning stage. I thought, "This may take a long time."

~~History~~ Hairstory

> *When you look good, you feel good, and darling,*
> *You look marvelous!*
> *You know who you are!*

—Billy Crystal as Fernando

"Four hun…"

I could feel myself drifting off…and inside my head a chorus of parts were all running around and screaming. No, no, no was all I heard as my eyes glassed over.

"...dred to six hundred hours," my therapist completed her sentence. I was only vaguely aware of her finishing it. It was only the second time I met with her as I was trying to figure out where my journey may lead. I had a friend who told me that seventy hours was enough for her.

Hopelessness was setting in. The time. The cost. The pain.

The question I asked was how long did she think it would take to remove my beard with electrolysis? After her response, I was too petrified to ask her about hair transplants.

It was the spring of 2009, and I had no idea whether I was on a path to transition. I had been to my first transgender conference in January 2009 and learned that nothing was impossible. Or so I thought. I met people who had transitioned, who had a variety of surgeries, and many of the doctors who perform them. It was a world I only dreamed existed, and I spent four days living in it. Living in it as Grace—full time, day and night.

For the first time in my life, I started going to a gender therapist for, what I hoped, would help me gain more clarity on what I wanted to do. I wanted to believe that nothing was impossible. I so wanted to believe.

This seemed like a roadblock.

The Characters of Billy Crystal

I am always puzzled why some of the characters that Billy Crystal has portrayed have had such meaning to me. We are both New York-raised baby boomers (he is about six months younger than me). In the mid-1970s, he was on prime time TV as Jody, on *Soap*, a gay character who would wear a dress. When I watched *Soap*, I was not sure whether to laugh or cry. I was newly married, and I knew that She was hiding just below my surface. She wanted out but could not dare to. Ignore, make fun, laugh on the outside was my choice. There was no choice about all the crying on the inside.

"You look marvelous!" The quote from the ongoing *SNL* character Fernando. It was even a song. "When You Look Good, You Feel Good!" This is how I felt when I cross-dressed. Hidden and secretive and on guard, it was the trip to fantasyland. No matter how momentary it would be, it was dreamlike and yes, marvelous. As a guy, I never felt that I looked good and therefore never felt good about myself. Much has changed since then.

In the two *City Slickers* films, Billy Crystal played Mitch and in one scene laments on being a middle-aged man. Oh, how he hit a trigger point when he said his hair doesn't grow where he wants it but grows where he doesn't want it. I was at this point in my life also, watching my hairline recede and trying to understand why hair was growing out of my ears.

Thank you, Billy Crystal.

I was not sure whether I would transition. I continued to deny my truth as I had for so long.

I made a decision to start hair removal and try to do it as fast as possible. After all, even if I did not transition, it would make cross-dressing easier. Seventy hours sounded like a great target. I ignored the reality that my friend had straight, wispy thin facial hair. I on the other had a curly, thick unruly beard that at sixty-two, was mostly gray and white, and grew in random directions. Even the follicles curled and made it difficult for the needles to get to the roots on a regular basis. Laser worked on the dark hairs, but this barely made a difference. I was scheduling sessions for two hours each week. I did it on late Friday afternoons and hid for the weekend as my face was inflamed and often looked like the surface of the moon for days. I am pretty sure that *she* kept driving me to do this, in spite of the pain. Today, I am glad that she did.

I was afraid that my transition could not occur until my beard was fully cleared. Luckily, on my journey, I met many trans women who told me that was not true. It took me a while to accept this but I am glad that I did not let my beard removal stop me from transitioning. I did start to believe that nothing is impossible once again.

I have been going to electrolysis for five years now. The total number of hours is crossing over 200. I am now at a point where I go once every four to five weeks for about thirty minutes. I am almost done. If back in 2009 my therapist had said 200 hours, I would have probably reacted in the same way. One of the major lessons that I have learned on this journey is patience.

On this journey, I have also had laser and electrolysis just about everywhere on my body. My back, my chest, my legs, my arms, armpits, and my butt. When I did make the decision to undergo reassignment surgery, it was also necessary to clear the "donor" area. Imagine the fun of that.

> *Gimme a head with hair, long beautiful hair*
> *Shining, gleaming, streaming, flaxen, waxen…hair…*
> *Flow it, show it, long as God can grow it, my hair*

—"Hair," James Rado and Gerome Ragni

As best I can remember, it was 1982. I was thirty-five years old. I had two kids, and there was another on the way. One day at work my boss made an innocent comment to me about how he could see skin on the top of my head. I still cannot believe how triggered I was. Perhaps this is a male rite of passage, but I was not prepared, and certainly the woman inside was set off in such a major way. I do not remember the details, but I sure know that my protectors lashed out and fired various insults right back at him. He looked at me as if I was nuts. I was.

I was in college in the late 1960s. The time of hippies, protests against the war in Vietnam, sit-ins at colleges, the summer of love, and *hair*. I lived at home and commuted from Brooklyn to Manhattan to school. I wanted to grow my hair, but the *unstated* rules at home held me back. There were no threats or spoken rules; it just seemed to me that it would not be accepted. This restriction had so much power over me. (What is it about the power of unspoken rules?)

My goal was to get my degree and get a job far from home. Twenty-two years living at home was enough. I was worried that with long hair I might not get a job as an engineer. An engineering degree was a ticket to a job that would pay the ungodly amount of almost $10,000 per year. I would keep my hair short for that. Not many of my classmates had long hair at this time. In the cafeteria, it was easy to tell the engineering students from the art/architecture students. The latter all had flowing locks of some sort. For some reason they seemed less clean than the engineering students, but that could have been my imagination. I always wondered if I would have ever been admitted into the art school, and if so, what journey that would have led me on.

I moved to the Boston area in 1969 after college and worked as an engineer. I learned how to design computers that navigated rockets. That's an entirely different story! It took until

1972 until I let my hair grow. I was still the odd one in the work environment even in the middle of Cambridge, Massachusetts.

In my forties, I was letting my hair grow and trying the old comb over trick. I was fooling myself.

By my late fifties I gave up and went for the buzz cut every four weeks.

Once I had the Big Closet, I bought many wigs. I hate wigs. But since I only cross-dressed in private it was more than enough.

I finally took a step outdoors when I was sixty-one and had to do something about my hair. I purchased two human hair custom hairpieces and dyed my hair, which I was letting grow out—at least where there was hair, a matching color. They looked fine, but I was far from satisfied.

I reached the point in my life where taking this leap was no longer a matter of choice. It was necessary. I spent years, no decades, hiding and in denial, not only to myself, but to everyone I ever knew. It was exhausting. It impacted every waking moment of my life. I could never answer the simple question, "Who am I?"

Two sides of the coin. Remove the hair you don't want, and replant hair you do want. Both need patience. Oh, so much patience. Parts of me wanted everything immediately. I learned to deal with them and exercise patience.

The years from 2009 through 2013 have been the years of decisions, action, and transition for me. Reaching self-acceptance of my true gender, I was faced with the question of what was I to do and at what cost? Sometimes I think it was like undertaking another degree program, to see if I can graduate and get my degree in being female.

2009

Live as if you were living a second time and as though you had acted wrongly the first time.

—Viktor E. Frankl

Skydivers and base jumpers look forward to jumping into the void. Perhaps they are adrenaline junkies and get a great rush both leading up to and during their flight through the air. The people who do this love their rush, but they are also secure in their skills and their equipment and they—I hope fully understand the risks they are taking and have a pretty good idea where they are planning to land.

I, too, was reaching the edge of a cliff and was preparing to take a leap. However, I did not have a parachute strapped to my back. No matter how much I was preparing to take this leap, I had no equipment, no security, and no idea where I would land.

I reached the point in my life where taking this leap was no longer a matter of choice. It was necessary. I spent years, no decades, hiding and in denial, not only to myself, but to everyone I ever knew. It was exhausting. It impacted every waking moment of my life. I could never answer the simple question, "Who am I?"

I was ready to take the leap to live authentically.

For me, achieving self-acceptance that I am transsexual and was ready to do something about it, this cliff was quite high; I had no idea where the ground was.

As I leaned over the edge (speaking metaphorically here) the question at hand was whether my life was ending or beginning or was the reality that it was both? I did not feel like a

Phoenix, triumphantly rising from the ashes of my previous being. After all, I was not a youngster, and I had lived a lot of life.

I could not turn back. I could no longer stay where I was. I had to leap.

I had already come out to my neighbors and my family just before I graduated in May. I told them that I was transgender and cross-dressed. I was honest and told them I had no idea where it would lead. There were various responses, but I did not lose anyone. So far, so good!

It was the night of the Halloween party at the club in late October 2009. I continued to wrestle with the question of whether or not I would or could transition.

I had on the red dress that Lieutenant Uhura wore in the original *Star Trek*. Geekiness is apparently gender independent. There were many people there, but there was one person who came in late and was dressed as a witch. Her name was Denise, and that night she became my muse, my teacher. She had transitioned and had surgeries. She was willing to share her stories. Most people left at 11:00 p.m. I and a few other women who were thinking about transitioning sat and listened and asked questions until 1:00 a.m. We were all mesmerized. Denise told us about her facial surgery and her reassignment surgery. Denise was also still married to her wife.

Denise offered to meet with any of us again. I took her up on her offer, and we became friends. She has been a great resource to me. I call her my muse.

I had met a post-op transsexual. She was a real person. I could talk to her and learn from her. Everything was sounding more possible.

A week later I got an email that I was—perhaps not so patiently—waiting for. It was early November 2009.

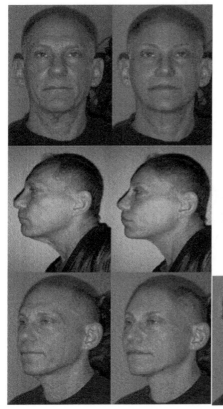

Three weeks earlier I sent three pictures of myself, of the male me, to a woman in the UK who had a business that she called Virtual FFS. FFS is short for facial feminization surgery. There are many plastic surgeons who specialize in transforming male facial characteristic to female ones.

I had known for a long time there would be no way that I could or would transition without FFS. Many people do, but I was six-ty-two years old and already becom-

Virtual FFS photos projecting before and after.

ing an old man, no matter what Tessa's comments were. I had no idea what could be done or how I would make a decision. No idea at all. For a little over one hundred dollars, the woman in the UK would take three pictures; a frontal, profile, and an angled side view of your face and Photoshop them with her recommendations on various procedures. She had many examples on her website so I thought that this would be a worthwhile investment.

Nervously, I opened the email to look at the pictures. I sent her three pictures and she returned four pictures. She updated each of the views I sent her, along with a full description of what she advised as changes and what procedures I could discuss with a real surgeon. They looked great. They certainly made me look twenty years younger. There was a significant amount of procedures she recommended including brow ridge shaving and scalp reduction, nose job, neck lift, eyebrow raising, and facelift. However, it was the fourth picture that had the largest impact to me. At first I did not realize it was a projection of me. It was the angled view picture that was morphed post-surgery but with added hair and makeup. It was the picture of a lovely young woman.

She took over the entire system in a flash. You have no more excuses, she yelled to anyone who was listening. She watched for any response, for any other part that wanted to argue with her. She watched and waited. She knew them all. One of her parts suggested that she check in with all the parts and make sure there was no resistance left. She thought this was a good idea. She checked; there were a few parts that were worried and afraid of how much it may hurt, but all the parts were on board. They all agreed; it was going to be her time.

He also knew it was time, and all the work he had done for such a long time was coming to an end. He closed his eyes and took a long, slow, and very deep breath. Then he said that he was OK with this also and volunteered to help with the planning. All of his inner friends knew this was coming, and they agreed it was time and joined in too.

Perhaps he wasn't such a bad guy after all, she thought.

I made a decision to take the next step. There were so many details. It was still pretty scary to think about. There were rules and steps. My therapist needed to know. I was on a slow path going nowhere until I walked into her office in November. Unlike many of my friends, I was very patient and only saw her once a month. I told her I was ready for hormones. She was surprised, and her initial response was that since I had only seen her about six or seven times so far, she had not got to this point. However, before I even needed to explain she looked at me and asked if I was certain. I said yes, and she said OK. I started hormones in January 2010.

Unintended Consequences

"Alice came to a fork in the road. 'Which road do I take?' she asked.
'Where do you want to go?' responded the Cheshire Cat.
'I don't know,' Alice answered.
'Then,' said the Cat, 'it doesn't matter.'"

—Lewis Carroll, Alice in Wonderland

Unconscious.

That's a fair way to describe how I lived most of my life. I wondered how many other people live their lives in this manner. I suspect that many do.

How many people choose a road that doesn't matter? They either do not know where they want to go or for some reason, perhaps many reasons, they have parts of themselves that block them from getting or worse, even knowing what they want. How many of us are really knowing and then living their truth?

I know how much I struggled with my parts and my truth around my gender identity for such a long time. It wasn't clear to me that people may well struggle with many issues in defining who they really are and how they want to be in the world. I suspect that there are those of us who have only an internal struggle that no one has any idea is going on. That was apparently true for me. When I came out, not a single person had any idea what my internal battle was all about. My protector parts did their jobs well in not letting anyone close enough where I would perhaps make a mistake and let them know what was going on inside me. My arrogant, obnoxious, know-it all parts provided a huge buffer to keep people away. I did have parts that were sad and lonely due to this, but they each had to deal with the burdens of the system.

I finally knew what I was going to do. I knew that I had to be prepared for losses and potential abandonment. I knew that my kids might perceive this change as a loss of their father. I hoped that this would not happen, but I was prepared to be responsible if they did.

I was not prepared for one impact that it had on my son Elie, and the resulting impact it had back on me. It put me on this mission that has led me to sharing my story with you.

I knew it was going to be very hard for me to tell the kids that I was transgender. I remember the last family meeting back in 2001, when I had to tell them that their parents were getting divorced. We all survived that experience. I was not certain what would survive after I told them my truth. I was not even sure how or when to tell them and also tell my ex, their mom.

My planning parts were confused. Do I write a letter and send it to them, tell them individually in person, get them together and tell them all at once? I really did not know where I was headed with all this being transgender at the time, but I was already going out dressed, even to shows downtown, with my girlfriends from school. Who knows who I might run into being out and about?

One Saturday afternoon I was driving to meet one of my girlfriends at her apartment to go to a show. I knew I would be driving by where my son and his wife lived. I was still driving the very recognizable truck that went on the 2001 road trip, and when I neared my son's block I saw him and his wife walking the dog. Grace was out, driving the truck. My heart just about blasted through my chest, as I shrank as low down in the driver's seat as I possibly could as I passed by where they were walking. I wondered if I was looking for trouble driving down this street. I wondered. I knew I had to come out to my family now.

I wrote a letter. I wanted to tell the kids independently of telling my ex. It was the right thing to do, and so often in the past I have not done the right thing. Elie and his wife were living in Tucson and were actually on a trip. When they returned, my ex was going out to visit them. The logistics were crazy. There was no good way to do this. I asked Stella, Simi, and his wife if I could meet up with them, as there was something I wanted to tell them. I set up with my ex to meet her for dinner, and I let Elie know that I needed to talk to him when he returned home but before his mom visited.

There was no easy way to say it. I was at Simi's house.

"I am transgender, and I struggled all my life with this. I go out dressed as a woman, and I have no idea where I am going with this, and yes, Tessa knows about it," I blurted out rapidly.

Silence with staring. Stella did not say another word the entire time I was there, and it took her a few weeks before we talked again. Simi said that was not what he was expecting, thinking more likely I would be telling them that I would be getting married. (That was not even a remote possibility.)

A week later I met with my ex-wife at a restaurant, and told her. Shock but not silence. She listened and talked but I had no idea what she was experiencing. I learned later she was experiencing a good deal.

It was another week until Elie got home and I could get on a phone call with him. I asked if the other kids had told him anything yet and he said no, but he was also clearly worried about an "I need to tell you something" call.

I blurted the same sentences to Elie on the phone. His response was totally different than the others. Without skipping a beat, as I finished my sentence, I heard back:

"That's great Dad, be whoever you are! That's awesome!"

It was my turn to be silent, trying to believe if I just heard what I heard.

We chatted some more, and he shared that he had a suspicion that I was going to tell him I had some terrible sickness, so my announcement of being *only* transgender was a relief. Interestingly, when I came out at work two years later there were a few people who had the same response.

I sent each of my family members a letter. I still do not know if they ever read it. I let them know that I did not believe in family secrets, and it was OK with me if they share with whomever they wanted to get support from, and they did not need to protect me. I was still taking baby steps in being out, but this was my journey. I just asked my family to start a new journey of their own, and did not want to put restrictions on them.

I closed the letter as with the following:

Simi, Stella, and Elie, no matter what happens I am and will always be your dad, and I love you guys with all my heart. I am now finding a way to love myself the same way.

Love to all,

Dad

Once again I could breathe. I had no idea what this would do to my relationships with my family. I really had jumped off the cliff, and was flying through the air. I really had no idea where, or if, I would land, and if I did, would I still be in one piece?

Perhaps there was a new normal forming, and although it took Stella a while before we would communicate again, things were OK. There was even a plan forming on when everyone would meet Grace.

I think it was a few months later that I first got an email from Elie. He wanted to talk to me about something. Uh oh, I was now going to be on the receiving end of something. I had a part saying, "Oh this is what it feels like!"

I answered the phone and Elie sounded a bit confused and agitated. He was telling me about how much he liked doing the different adventures that he did. He ran marathons, he biked Centuries, and camped and loved being outside. He said that it seemed like his life was feeling out of balance and was trying to figure out what he wanted to be. He shared that he had a nice house and a great job, but there was something that felt not fully complete and there was much more to himself, and he was starting to feel somewhat constrained.

I was listening and starting to panic and so wanted to be there for him. The old Dad-in-Charge part was woken from a long sleep, but just hovered around trying to get as much information as he could.

Elie shared with me that after I explained how long I hid my own gender issues and struggled so long with them, he has been thinking about what is important to him.

He then told me: "I don't want to get to be your age and realize I went down the wrong path in life!"

There are moments in life when time seems to stop, and then, everything changes. This was one of those moments. I had not yet even known where my journey was going to take me. I thought my journey was mine alone. I had no idea that even the sharing of my journey so far, would have an impact on someone else, let alone my son. It was both difficult to fathom and yet immediately understood. Hearing my story made Elie look into his story and ultimately his truth, and he was now struggling to figure it out and find the right road.

I learned that expressing my truth encourages others to do the same. Is this where my own journey is leading me? Is this a mission for me? It sure felt like that.

As Viktor Frankl said in *Man's Search for Meaning*:

Everyone has his own specific vocation or mission in life; everyone must carry out a concrete assignment that demands fulfillment. Therein he cannot be replaced, nor can his life be repeated. Thus, everyone's task is unique as is his specific opportunity to implement it.

I helped Elie sort through some of his feelings and encouraged him to find a therapist. With help from his wife, his best friend, a therapist, and me, Elie was able to sort through his feelings and right his ship. He is now living a life of adventures with his wife and dogs, always pushing to further understand his truth. Again, they teach me so much.

It was an unintended consequence of my own long journey. In addition to my own journey yet to be traveled, I had another mission assigned to me. One that demands fulfillment.

Simi and Stella were already on their journeys that were off the beaten trail. As a parent I always wanted my kids to find their own path to happiness. As I struggled through my own life, with no one knowing of the struggle, it was hard for me to answer a common question asked of parents: what are your dreams for your kids? I wanted them to figure their lives out, wherever that will take them. Do I worry about them? Do I want them to be happy? Of course I do, but I learned that only they will know the answers for them, and I may or may not understand their choices in life. Thinking I know what is right for them has gone away with the Dad-in-Charge part. Dad-the-Friend hopes to be an advisor and supporter. Even if Dad is now Grace.

Stella has a BA in French and an MA in Special Education but chose to go to the Farm School in Orange, Massachusetts and is now a farmer. Simi has a BA in Environmental Studies and has become an award-winning photographer and is a stay-at-home dad. Perhaps my entire family has learned to live their truth.

Getting Ready

And the day came when the risk to remain tight in a bud was more painful than the risk it took to blossom.

—Anais Nin

She had been fighting for a long, long time, and now the fight was over. She dreamed of this day but never thought that it would happen. She was excited, and there was a sense of wonder, as she reflected back on all the years, all the hiding, and all the battles that no one ever saw. She thought about all her inner friends that helped to guide her and protect her on the path to this day, and how glad she was to have them with her. Without them, she would have probably done something impulsive that may not have turned out well. She was glad that she learned to listen to them—even if it was hard for her, and to learn patience. Even now, even with the next path clear, she knew there would be many choices and many crossroads to choose from.

She was glad that he was now on board, too. He and many of his manager friends were so good at planning and adjusting to problems and issues when they arose. She hoped they would really help her now, as she knew she and her friends were not nearly as good as they were at these tasks.

She had won. She knew what she wanted. She was going to be free and living in the world each and every day. But she knew it would not happen today, no, not quite yet. There was so much to do, and she needed to plan. She had so much to learn if she was really going to succeed, and she needed all the help she could get. The parts that always advised patience smiled and knew that she would be fine.

Deep down, he knew this day would come. Some of his inner friends were always learning all they could so they would be prepared for helping with the transition if and when needed. These parts loved planning all sort of options and those crazy what-if situations. They thought it was fun and reflected back to the old Boy Scout motto of *Be Prepared!* He thought they never stopped thinking and planning. This was fine. It was always harder for him to deal with the worrying and fearful parts. They were the ones that would get out of control and take over everything. Even now, they were muttering with each other, and he had to keep reassuring them that everything is fine, and it will be OK working with her.

He knew he was really tired of fighting her. He finally realized he no longer knew what he was fighting for.

"This is the right thing to do, but let's all do it the right way," he advised each and every part in the system.

She was watching and listening to this exchange. Yes, definitely, he was not a bad guy at all. She was learning to like him — to like him a lot.

The World Professional Association for Transgender Heath (WPATH) has created guidelines called the Standards of Care (SOC) that most (but not all) medical, clinical, and other professionals will follow as they help evaluate and guide gender variant clients to "achieve lasting personal comfort with their transgender selves." These guidelines include the need for an evaluation prior to transition and living a "real life test" in, what I will call, the true gender for one year before receiving a recommendation for any genital reassignment surgery. Most doctors also advise their patients to take hormones for about two years to achieve their maximum breast growth before considering breast augmentation. Following these guidelines required more patience.

I made the decision. I was going to transition. The only defined step I was going to take was to start taking hormones. I had no idea what impact that would have on me. Sure, skin softening, breast growth, and emotional changes were all listed as results. I had not met too many women yet who had gone down this road, so I really did not have a lot of first-hand data. I did have one friend from Tiffany Club who was moving so fast through her transition, it both scared and inspired me. Each time I heard her talk about what she was doing, I had so many mixed feelings.

"Yes, I want what she's having," was fighting with, "Take it slow, that's not your journey." It seemed like these parts were in a wrestling match endlessly circling around each other with neither making a first move. I was sure that the Take-It-Slow part would win, so I let them both enjoy their little dance.

I had intention. I would transition. I had no plan, no time-line. Hormones would be the first baby step on the new road.

The road would have a few rocks in it.

As it turned out, they weren't that far away.

2010

My therapist recommended and sent an introductory letter to a doctor who would provide hormones for me. I was so excited to take this step. During the physical I was asked what I wanted.

Perhaps I should have not let the Take-It-Slow part leave their dance, as the I-Want-It-Now! part took over and asked for everything, before I even knew what happened. I got scripts for an androgen blocker, spironolactone; finasteride, normally a drug used to reduce an enlarged prostrate but has a side effect that improves male pattern baldness; and Estradiol (I chose to use transdermal patches as they were supposed to be easier on the liver). I started to use them early in January 2010 and was so excited.

I was so happy and did not realize that at that first appointment my excitement must have filled the room (I can do that sometimes), and the doctor made an error. I failed to get a baseline of my blood work.

Every morning I would wake up and hope that I would see breast growth. I think I was hoping to see a millimeter difference. No matter. I was flying high.

One month later I went for a check in and all was fine, so I set up another appointment for early March. The appointment was on a Monday morning, and I was still feeling great, and I asked if I could increase the estradiol, and added a second patch each week. They did blood work at this appointment, and I went off happy once again.

The following Friday night I was out at a trans friendly, local coffee house with a bunch of friends from the club. It was a lovely evening with great live music and a welcoming crowd, which was so much fun. It was a little after nine when my phone rang, and I saw my doctor's name pop up. Oh my! I had to answer it. The doctor said that my blood work reports showed that my liver enzyme numbers were much too high and that I should immediately stop the hormones and come in so they could check me next week. The doctor admitted that there had been a mistake, and there was no baseline report, so stopping would be the best course of action.

I was panicked and pissed and not sure which feeling was stronger. I told the friends I was with, and they expressed so much empathy and concern. This was another new feeling for me to take in.

Thoughts rushed through my mind: I had the blood work done early in the week. I was getting this call now, late on a Friday night! What does this mean? How can this happen? No hormones! How can I continue? Liver enzymes are high—whatever this means—is it bad? I did not know what to think!

I called my therapist and left a message on her machine. I was pretty scared but put on a happy face with my friends and made the best of the rest of the evening. I had a part that knew it was the right thing to do. Inside me there was a fire drill going on.

I was aware of people who get hormones over the Internet or by other methods and administer them on their own. There are so many stories of trans women who have no other way and are so hidden and so hurting. This may be their only choice. I believed it was dangerous. I could not understand how I was doing everything right and then this occurs. I needed to get those what-if-planner parts to work.

My therapist called me back on Saturday. I found a different doctor and luckily got an appointment a few weeks later. This time I went to an endocrinologist who had lots of experience with cross-gender hormones. The exams were thorough. After one month off of all hormones, my baseline levels were back in an acceptable range. I restarted the hormones, although on a less aggressive plan. No more finasteride; lower doses of spiro and estradiol.

I got past the bump in the road and went on to enjoy the summer.

Tessa and I had a great summer biking, and we took our regular week in Ogunquit and also went to Chicago where we also biked. Deep down, I was pretty sure this might well be the last time we would be doing this.

As summer drifted into fall, I was happy with the little bit of breast growth I observed and felt great. I still did not have a plan, and was wrestling with how I would pay for the various procedures if and when I decided to take the next step. I was working the dual jobs—fulltime days in the tech word and a few nights at the clinic. The money from the clinic was paying for my electrolysis each week, which was great, but I might have to pull money out of retirement funds if I wanted to move forward.

My what-if parts were doing their jobs and had a thought.

It was a Sunday afternoon in October, and I was settling down to watch football on TV. I was aware that the week before the Human Rights Campaign (HRC) announced new requirements for their Corporate Equality Index (CEI) for 2011. The new rules would require companies to have some form of transgender health benefits if they hoped to receive a 100 percent rating. I decided to write a long letter to the senior VP of human resources at my company—someone I had never met, and only knew by name. I introduced myself as Grace Stevens and that I was transgender and would be transitioning in the workplace in 2011. I said that it was not my real name—yet, and then I explained all the reasons why the company should institute transgender benefits. The letter was six pages long. I finished, looked it over, and took a big deep breath. I hit send and settled down to watch the Patriots football game.

Within a half hour, I had a return email. It was Sunday afternoon. I had not expected a response this quickly. Tentatively I opened it. With only had three sentences, it said:

"Dear, Grace,

You will have a difficult journey. The company will be happy to take care of you on it. I will have the benefits person contact you."

I could not believe what just happened. What would I do now? Over the next three months, I worked closely with the benefits people and the Chief Diversity Officer, and the company announced that starting in January 2011, they would officially provide some transgender benefits. I was going to be the first to receive them.

What was I going to do?

2011

She could have never done all the work those planner parts were doing. They organized all the meetings with the different surgeons at the First Event 2011 conference. They proposed a plan. Name change at the end of March, and facial surgery the end of April followed by a month out of work for recovery and then return to work as Grace. For the clinic, the plan was to take off about three months before returning.

They really were amazing, she thought, as she realized how great they managed.

Then, hiding in the background a part appeared to be crying. She called over and asked it why it was so sad. It was the lonely part that always wanted connection and was so afraid to speak up. Sobbing and slowly it came over to her. The part felt so bad and worried that they may lose Tessa in the transition.

She really didn't know how to comfort that part, because she felt the same way.

In 2010, the First Event conference underperformed financially, which created revenue issues for The Tiffany Club. By 2010, I was a member of the board of the club and the treasurer. I was worried and convinced a few other people to help me take over as co-chairs for First Event 2011. We reworked the budget, raised prices, and lowered expenses. We also started to seek out donations and sponsorships. This new team of four co-leaders was able to turn the conference around and provide a decent profit that was able to support the club for another year. As one of the co-leaders, I was on the floor of the conference from Wednesday through Sunday from 8:00 a.m. to 1:00 a.m. each day and got a limited amount of sleep. Three of the four co-leaders have now done this each year since, and although we did not really know what we were doing in 2011, we are pretty good at organizing and running and growing a conference. One of my old arrogant parts had now become quite adept at customer service. Grace was becoming very visible in the local community. So much for hiding.

The plan was in place. The Chief Diversity Officer set up a meeting with the President and a group of VPs, most of whom I knew and had worked with. Since there were over 1000 people on the campus, I thought that it would be best to let the senior management team know about my transition beforehand so that they would be able to handle any issues that might eventually trickle up to them. The look on their faces when the Chief Diversity Officer walked in the room with me was priceless. I rather bluntly announced that I was transgender and in about a month I would be leaving for facial surgery and returning as Grace. I had written a six-page letter explaining all the details and handed to them. A few asked some questions; a few mentioned their support; one said his wife's best college friend transitioned female to male, and a few were silent and looked like deer caught in the headlights. I walked out with an agreement of confidentiality and their support.

Over the next few days, I met with my supervisor and a dozen peer level managers, and they also were supportive and agreed to confidentiality. Some of these people I worked with every day, and it was really awesome to be able to continue our relationships as I was on this part of my journey. Individually I was able to share a good deal with them before I went off. When I went off on vacation for four weeks, many people could not figure out what was happening to me, as there was no information given to them. They did not get information until a week before my return as Grace, when my therapist was hired to come in and do diversity training about my transition for about 200 people.

On March 25, 2011, I legally changed my name. I waited for about an hour in the courtroom. When called up to the judge, he asked if the name change was my choice. I responded affirmatively. He checked that my divorce was long ago finalized and that I did not owe any money to anyone, and then signed the order. It took no more than one minute. I floated out of the courtroom.

The Last Night of the World

I learned as a child not to trust in my body
I've carried that burden through my life
But there's a day when we all have to be pried loose
If this were the last night of the world
What would I do?

—"The Last Night of the World," Bruce Cockburn

What would I do? I had to take care of myself. This was very clear to me. Finally! But there was going to be a cost that I did not want to think about.

It did not take much prodding for Tessa to remind me that when I first shared my secret with her, I told her that I would never transition. I cannot even remember how many times I said that to myself, let alone to her. Denial for me was operating both internally and externally. Although the journey for each of us is unique, I have seen both in others and myself that when we reach the point of self-acceptance of being trans-sexual, we focus so greatly on our own journey and not the impact on others we are with and who are with us in a relationship. I have learned that by choosing to take our own journey, we often unknowingly force many of the people in our lives to take their own journey, which they may not want to take and are most likely not well prepared to take. Our own self-focus, which may appear to others as selfishness, may well blind us to the impact on others.

I had been so focused on and excited about plans and my transition that I was not really a good friend and paying attention to the impact it would on have my friendship with Tessa. Perhaps what was worse, I was not able to be there to listen and provide any support for her. For me, I was choosing love over fear. The fear for me was the damage it would cause to or the end of our friendship. There were still parts of me that would not let me even think about it.

She was getting ready. This was going to be the last day that she had to be hidden. She expected the journey to be physically painful but knew it would be worth it all. This was going to be his last night in the world. After all the years, she was hoping to wake up in the hospital and perhaps finally hear the words, "It's a girl!" Even if it didn't come from outside of her, she knew those would be the first conscious words she would tell herself.

He was taking on so many new jobs and was really trying to console the lonely part that was so afraid of losing the connection with Tessa. There were so many other parts that were also there looking to him for reassurance as they watched her floating in a bubble of happiness. Finding words was difficult for him, as it always had been, but his strong and quiet presence and the fact that he was no longer fighting her were perhaps providing more support than words could ever do. Internally the system was finding a new sense of peace. His smile was the reassurance many of the parts latched on to.

It was a strange evening when I went to Tessa's. Neither of us had words to describe what we were feeling or what would come next. We were happy in each other's company, as we had been for so long. There were plenty of tissues as we quietly took turns crying without words to explain. We really did not know what, if anything, the future held for us. We still had our plans for a vacation in August, but we both agreed that we would see if this still may occur. As with most of our time together, we just said this would be "as long as this makes sense for each of us."

I know in my head that it was hard for Tessa, but on that night I had no ability to express empathy as I was so focused on my own journey. This was not usual in our friendship, as we both were typically present for each other in our times of stress and need. This evening was very different. Not many words were spoken, but emotions were leaking out everywhere.

I cried as I drove home that night and so hoped I had not lost my best friend. I knew I would not have made it to this point without her in my life and wondered if I was about to cross into a new world where I may never see her again.

The Brave New World

It was about eighteen months since I made the decision to climb to the top of the mountain and take the leap. It was the time to jump.

I needed to be at the hospital at 6:00 a.m. for facial surgery. It was Thursday, April 28, 2011. I asked Simi to drop me off and then pick me up the next day. Afterwards he said this was one of the hardest things he has ever done, especially to see me swollen and bandaged when he picked me up.

This surgery was the marking point of my transition. Larnie went in, and Grace came out. As they administered the anesthesia, I was thinking about ends and beginnings, and wondering where this journey would take me, as I was saying good-byes to many of my parts.

I woke up and had to pee. My bladder felt like it was going to burst. It was a rough night, as a side effect of nine hours of anesthesia was urinary retention. It took until the middle of the next day before I had a catheter inserted to empty my bladder. I ended up needing one for two weeks. This was an unexpected part of the adventure.

One eye was swollen closed, and my entire face was bandaged and looked like a balloon overfilled and was ready to pop. Simi picked me in the late Friday afternoon and took me home. He was kind enough to sleep on my couch that night, and left early in the morning. I was taking a Percocet about every three hours.

When Simi left, I sat on the couch. The "I" that sat there was Grace!

She was sitting on the couch. *SHE* was sitting on the couch! She could not keep all her thoughts straight for too long as she drifted between pain and alertness, but she was the one that was sitting there, and more than just that lonely voice. She remembered that day so long ago when she tried to yell, "It is not a boy! I am a girl!" She thought that today was like doing it all over and it would be clear to everyone that today, "It's a girl!"

Before and after FFS surgery.

All the prep team parts were glad she was home now. They had set up a plan that *he* would have never let them do before. They knew he would never ask anyone for help or support. He did not want to appear weak or let anyone too close. All those cultural forces really had a strong impact on him, they thought. They understood that women will generally ask for help and support, so they thought this would be a great time to see how that worked. They knew that she would be home for the weekend and probably not be in the greatest shape. They asked four friends to take two-hour shift, to come stay and keep her company over the weekend. Only one of the four women friends she asked for help was a trans woman, and they all were happy to help, and glad to be asked, and said so. Wow, that felt so new; they smiled at each other.

Two came on Saturday and two on Sunday. She talked a bit and fell asleep a bit, but she really loved that she had friends. Real, breathing, walking friends, who were willing to help take care of her.

The fourth day after surgery was the worst day of all. I had a fair amount of bone work on my jaw and on the fourth day it turned black and blue and hurt. I was surprised by this delayed reaction but learned afterwards that it's not atypical. As I sat, slept, popped some percs for the pain, a realization brought clarity to me. I had transitioned. It did not matter that I had not dressed in the past four days or that my head was fully covered with compression bandages; I was now Grace all the time. I was only beginning to heal, but I now knew that the next set of surgeries—reassignment surgery was now clearly something that I wanted to do as soon as I could. One week earlier I had no clarity or plan as to this part of my journey. But four days after facial feminization surgery (FFS), it was clear that in a year, I would have gender reassignment surgery (GRS).

I was black and blue until about day twenty when I could go out and look half decent. On day twenty-one post-surgery, I got a new driver's license with a new picture and an "F" under the gender marker. I smiled a lot now.

I returned to work on May 31, 2011. I was a bit nervous as I parked my car and walked through the door, climbed the stairs, and walked down the hall to my office. There was a new nameplate on the door: Grace Stevens. I walked up to my boss's office and introduced Grace to him. He was awesome. He told me about the trainings the week before. As people came by they were pretty amazed by how I looked, as at the training they were warned that I might be pretty bruised from the surgery. Over the next few days, so many people came by to say hello, and to tell me how brave and courageous I was. This made me very uncomfortable. I did not feel brave or courageous. I felt that I had no choice but to do what I had done.

Most of the women were all over me to chat and complimented me on my clothes and told me it was so much easier to talk and share with me than just a month earlier. There was a mixed response from the males. A few told me that I looked good and commented that even they were surprised they could say that. Most were curious and civil although almost everyone had trouble using my new name, and it took one to two months for some people. It seemed to bother them more than it bothered me. I found it interesting rather than bothersome. One person told me that I was his third trans acquaintance. He was at two other companies where a co-worker had transitioned. I was pretty amazed to hear that.

The most amazing thing was that I received an email from a woman in the company whom I did not know. She said that she had transitioned in another company but no one knew about her history. She wanted to meet me. I was so honored by this and had a fabulous conversation with her. Transitioning in the day job went well.

In August, I planned to return to the clinic. I, myself, went to train all the other clinicians. They were awesome. One of my colleagues was one of the friends who had helped me that first weekend after surgery. When I start up new groups, I am just introduced as Grace. No one has ever said anything over the past few years since I transitioned.

Also in August, Tessa and I went on our usual vacation to Ogunquit. It was a hard for her, as she thought people were looking at me and wondering, but we were still friends. I considered myself very blessed.

In October, my first granddaughter was born. I was there with the extended family and fully accepted by all. Did I say I was blessed?

In 2011, I was sixty-four years old when I transitioned my gender.

2012

We were getting the hang of planning and running First Event. The conference was starting to grow and more volunteers joined us.

I met and talked to the surgeon I had chosen for my reassignment surgeries in April and September, and set the dates. In 2011, all the surgeries and all the transition activities were public affairs. In 2012, it was private and the details were invisible to all others. It was meaningful to me and me alone. Again, I took four weeks off from work, but there was no training, no wonder, and no big unveiling upon my return. For the past year, people had commented behind my back how happy Grace was. It was true, and apparently it showed. As far as work was concerned, Grace did her job, and when I returned, people were glad to have me back.

By choosing to do my surgery in the spring, I knew that I would probably be giving up most of my summer bicycling. I knew I would miss it. My first surgery was in early April, and I really was not in decent condition until mid-August and then had another surgery planned after Labor Day. Tessa was now starting to bike faster than me, and even though I knew why, I didn't like it very much. Now I don't have as many excuses as she has become faster and better. Perhaps I am just getting old.

From April 2011 through September of 2012, I underwent nineteen hours of surgery to align my body to what my brain knew forever. There was still more to do.

I am not sure that it is true, but I heard that hair transplant procedure can be impacted by shock of surgery and anesthesia. Although I wanted to do hair transplants years earlier, the best advice I received was to wait until all the major surgeries are completed. On November 1, 2012, I had my first procedure, with another that followed six months later. This required patience, as I was told that coverage might well take twelve to eighteen months, which turned out to be accurate.

Through this all, I was still going to electrolysis.

At the end of September 2012, the project I was working on was cancelled. I updated my resume and started to worry.

2013

The last three months of 2012 were marked by having nothing to do at work. My company eliminated a number of jobs in early October, but even though it was not clear what I was doing, my job was not in that group. Tessa still reminds me how miserable I was during this time.

I wrestled with my resume. My entire work and school history was not under the name of Grace Stevens. When (not if) a potential employer sees a resume and knows someone at one of the companies listed, they will often "backdoor" you, and see if someone knows you. No one would know Grace Stevens in any of the positions listed. There was no good solution. I had two versions of my resume. One explained that I was trans and had transitioned; one did not. I had no real criteria where I sent them. I never received responses from any resumes I sent out.

On February 4, 2013 my job was eliminated. I was not surprised. There were around sixty people let go that day, so I do not believe that I was singled out for any reason. I believe that I was the oldest person let go. The thought of finding another job filled me with worries about being too old, too expensive, and possibly too trans. Each is, on its own, a subtle issue. Taken together, I was concerned and overwhelmed.

On the morning of February fifth, the alarm no longer rang.

Between severance and potential unemployment insurance, I did not have any immediate financial issues and although I would be turning sixty-six in August I really was not ready to retire. In some strange sense, Grace was only turning two!

In mid-March, one of the other co-leaders of First Event and I went to another transgender conference, the Keystone Conference in Harrisburg, Pennsylvania, to see how it was run. The people there were fabulous hosts to us, and we had a wonderful time attending workshops and dinners. We never get to relax like that at First Event as we are always nonstop busy. I have learned that managing a conference is a 24/7 job during the conference. It is fun, and we have a huge impact on people's lives, but for us, it can be draining.

On the Saturday night at Keystone, after most of the conference activities were completed, I went into the bar and met up with one of the doctors and her husband whom I had become friendly with. We ended up chatting from 11:00 p.m. to 1:00 a.m., as I shared my dilemma about having no idea what I should do about my job situation.

Once again, I had been provided with a new pair of muses, who suggested and encouraged me to create a training business to teach people about gender and gender variance. My background in the corporate world and as a mental health counselor coupled with my personal experience of transitioning in two work places, along with leading a transgender conference for a number of years, they thought I would be a natural. It resonated with me immediately. I floated out of the bar, went to bed, but really could not sleep that night.

I had thought that when I transitioned in 2011, I was done with reinventing myself. This turned out to be not the case. By May of 2013, I had a new website online, and started a consulting business that I named *Gender Variance Education and Training*. I was networking with everyone I knew and made cold calls to other people to introduce myself. I was introduced to someone who was a member of the National Speakers Association and started to go to their monthly meetings. Through networking there, I got my first paid training for the senior human resources team at a large local bank. I went back to Lesley University, my alma mater, and held a training session for graduate counseling students, and also, two colleagues from the therapist community invited me to conduct training for the groups or clinics they worked with.

By the end of the year, the Chief Diversity Officer at the company where I used to work called and hired me for training in Kentucky where a member of the staff was transitioning.

I also had the opportunity to go into a regional high school and talk with a gay straight alliance (GSA) of students and teachers. In the school that year, there were four trans-identifying students. I had no agenda and just went to encourage them all to live their truth, as this was the mission that I received after my experience with Elie. After the talk, I learned that for many of the students, I was the first transgender adult they had met. I loved the thank you notes I received.

I did not work a lot, but I learned that I loved training and speaking and sharing my journey with others. Apparently this made a difference to them.

I learned something very interesting this year. During the year, I have run into a few people months after I initially spoke or presented to them. More often than not, they tell me that they remember my story or often think about what I have been through. I was very pleasantly amazed.

Oh, before I forget, Tessa and I biked a lot all summer and even added some hilly terrain. We biked in Martha's Vineyard, Tanglewood, and up to Franconia Notch in the White

Mountains of New Hampshire. Our regular August trip to Maine included a few rides of over thirty-five miles each. Tessa is getting really strong. I don't know how much longer I can keep up with her. I also had a chance to ride the Cape Cod rail trail for fifty miles with Elie and Simi. Even without a job, it would be foolish for me to complain.

Elie had always told me that I should tell my story and write about it. I had a few parts that thought I did not have that much to say. They started to realize they just might be wrong.

Who Is a Hero?

"Perhaps some of us have to go through dark and devious ways before we can find the river of peace or the highroad to the soul's destination."

—Joseph Campbell, *The Hero with a Thousand Faces*

Over the past few years, it has struck me how often people's response to learning I am transgender is a form of: *you are so brave, you are so courageous!* Many times it is followed by: *I could never do that.*

I have heard the same experience from other trans women and trans men. We also find that a common response to this is: "Be thankful that you didn't have to."

This bothers me in that it seems to negate our own life's experience and not honor ourselves. I suspect their comments that they could never do what we have chosen to do is issued by one of their own parts, of fear and lack of understanding, as to just how important aligning our outward facing life with our inner life of knowing our truth is to us. If they have never experienced this dissonance that transgender people do, how could they know? They can't. Once again, for each of us, our stories, and our journeys are unique. People will make assumptions and try to simplify what they hear. I certainly know how fast my protector parts will take me over. You probably know from your own experiences how quickly you can be triggered and suddenly say something, and you do not even understand how it came out of your mouth.

I am learning that most people mean well, and I thank them. I suspect that they probably have many experiences that if they shared with me, I might not understand and be amazed at how brave and courageous they are.

Perhaps a better response would be, "Thank you so much. That is so kind of you to share with me. I am sure that you, too, have the courage to live your truth."

He was resting now. He was OK in his new job as a librarian of memories, and glad that he was no longer working nonstop 24/7. He had done this for sixty-four years. He thought he was always doing the right thing. He kept everything in balance as well as he could. He didn't always succeed. There were so many others around him, all thinking they knew what was best. He remembered how He tried so hard to control them but most of the time he failed.

He could now admit to himself that He always loved her and really, was always trying to protect her. He knew it hardly ever appeared that way. She was always so clear in knowing who she was. He always wished he had some clarity like hers. He was always so scared and did what he thought was best. He watches her now and is so glad that she is happy and learning how to be! He never had the chance for this.

He loves when she comes by to chat about old memories. She hid so much and for so long, and she knows there are so many pieces missing for her that he has access to. They really are becoming friends.

The more she got to know him, the more amazed she became. She remembered all those years when she battled with him. She wasn't sure when she realized that he really was not the enemy. He was never the enemy.

He told her many stories of the things he had done to make sure neither she nor any of the other parts would get hurt. She remembered some of these, and how angry she was at the time. She had no idea that he was trying to protect her. She was learning that he had struggled mightily on how to live in the world while dealing with all that was going on inside. She knew how hard her battle inside was, but his was so much bigger, really having to balance the two worlds. She did not even begin to appreciate how he did it.

She began to understand how brave he really was. How courageous he was for such a long time.

He was becoming her hero.

She told him this. He smiled.

LIVING MY TRUTH

It is never too late to be what you might have been.

—George Eliot

Dreamers

You're never given a dream without also being given the power to make it true.

— Richard Bach, *Illusions: The Adventures of a Reluctant Messiah*

The quote "It's never too late to be who you might have been," is widely attributed to George Eliot.

George Eliot was a Victorian era writer. I first heard the author's name when I had to read *Silas Marner* in high school. Honestly, I do not remember anything at all about that book. However, I learned that George Eliot was the pen name of Mary Ann Evans. The story goes that in that era, women could not become published writers and often took on male pen names.

Although nothing about the book was memorable to me, I did obsess about the idea of the author changing genders—at least in name.

This quote stayed with me for many years. I had dreams that someday, maybe, I might get to be who I truly am. Someday! Maybe? In my sixties, someday, maybe started to become real.

The question, "Who might have I been?" has been replaced by an even better question, "Who am I now?"

I had more dreams than just being a woman out in the world. They were so deeply buried, and I was not certain I knew how to access them. All the protection, all the years of drifting off, of not wanting to dream the impossible dreams.

The dreams to belong, to have friends and companions, to be able to tell jokes and stories were all blocked by parts that thought the risk was too great. It was another paradox. I isolated myself due to the fear of being isolated by others.

If they really knew me—if they knew I was not the big, loud, know-it-all man that they saw day in and day out, but really a sensitive woman trying to figure out how to just be in the world, it was clear they would all abandon me. So very, very clear.

Yet, there were many nights I would cry myself to sleep hoping to dream that someday, maybe the day when I could live my truth would arrive. When that day arrived, I could then go out into the world without fear, without needing to hide, and perhaps figure out who I am now.

In *Man of La Mancha*, Don Quixote sings in *The Impossible Dream:*

And I know if I'll only be true
To this glorious quest
That my heart will lie peaceful and calm
When I'm laid to my rest

I knew I was so much more than just my gender. We all are. But this so occupied my every waking moment. What else, who else am I? I transitioned. My biggest dream came true. Yes, my heart has become peaceful and calm, but I am not anywhere near ready to be laid to my rest. I have so much to be.

When Dreams Come True, Then What?

After I transitioned, I started going to improvisation workshops. I was afraid to go before I transitioned, as I had parts that were worried about what, in the spur of the moment, would come out. Now I was concerned that I had no idea who Grace was and wanted to give her space to find her voice. It was scary and hard. I started to attend these in early 2012, after my transition but before my gender reassignment surgery. In each of the workshops, I came out to the other attendees during introductions and shared that I had no idea what would come out of me, but I needed the space if it touched on my gender journey. No one ever had an issue with this, and I did hear many of the brave and courageous comments in reply. This reaction was fine as I was getting used to it and thanked them. This was a safe space for Grace to explore.

No matter what your journey is, if you are hiding parts of yourself, and getting tired of it, I highly recommend doing some improvisational work. You may be surprised at what you learn.

I was in an improvisation class the day before I flew out for my reassignment surgery. The classes are usually held in a medium auditorium space rented in a local church. The space this weekend had posters all around, and one was about living your dreams. I was staring at the poster for the first day and most of the second day, as I thought so much about how I was living my dream each day. Without much planning, I was inspired to get up in front of the group and start improvising a monologue; I really did not know what was about to come out.

I had already transitioned. This was Grace, female presenting Grace, who was already living her dearest dream. I don't remember the exact words, but it was something like this:

Look at the poster on the wall. How many people have their dreams come

> I have learned to dream again. I am dreaming of teaching and speaking and now writing. I am free in living my truth and sharing my truth with others. I get to be me, each and every moment. I no longer spend the energy hiding who I truly am.

true? Have you? Tomorrow I will be getting on a plane and flying to a place where I will fulfill a dream that I never thought possible. I will have the surgery that will align my body with my brain. This dream has been with me as long as I can remember — over sixty years — and impacted every part of my life.

In two weeks when I fly back home, what will I do? Are my dreams now over? What do you do after your dreams come true? Is this the end? Or, is it a beginning? This dream that is coming true is mine, and mine alone. It is not one easy to share, and I hope it will bring me the peace I have been dreaming about for so long. If it does, what is next?

(I looked slowly into the eyes of each attendee…as I said)…

What do you do when all your dreams come true?

(I took in a long slow breath and looked all around the room…then I added…)

Perhaps I need to dream some new dreams.

I have learned to dream again. I am dreaming of teaching and speaking and now writing. I am free in living my truth and sharing my truth with others. I get to be me, each and every moment. I no longer spend the energy hiding who I truly am. My story made a difference to at least one of my children and encouraged him and told him that it was OK to follow his dreams.

I never used to dream about having a mission and being able to a make an impact on others. It seemed to just happen to me. Today I dream about how to share it with others. I believe you can make your dreams come true too.

The Other Side of the Rainbow

Where troubles melt like lemon drops
Away above the chimney tops
That's where you'll find me
Somewhere over the rainbow bluebirds fly
Birds fly over the rainbow, why then oh why can't I?

"Over the Rainbow," Lyrics by Yip Harburg

She really was not quite sure when things changed. One day she noticed how much quieter it was. There were fewer parts hustling around inside and much less chatter. Every now and then there was still the Critic and the Judge popping up with complaint after complaint, but she had learned to be very soft and reassuring with them as they agreed to back off and just keep an eye on everything. When they made a good point, she thanked them and tried to learn from it. She wasn't sure they ever got used to being acknowledged like that as they grumbled off and chattered to themselves on the side.

She went exploring to find out why it was so much quieter. She had to go check on her new friend and see if he had any idea what was going on. He was still pretty much on top of everything.

"I hope that it is not a problem for you," he offered, when she shared what she was noticing.

"No, I was just wondering what has happened, and when? I was not even aware how much was changing," she said.

He laughed and told her that since she is spending so much time just being herself in every moment and it appears that no matter what happens now, she no longer goes into any type of panic, that he and so many of the parts that were so vigilant, to protect the system, no longer have to do those old jobs. The parts that were on guard each day 24/7, where they watched everything and everyone, and would not let anything pass through them without a thorough investigation as to the risk assessment, no longer do that job. They are now taking turns just walking around and checking in with all the other parts on a regular basis. They are in semiretirement and for the first time just getting a chance to relax and meet whoever else is in the system. They are enjoying the new friendships they are making.

She learned that they now have modeled themselves on security guards that walk around a building and punch in at the various stations to ensure they check all the areas. Compared to standing at the front gates with their rifles over their shoulders, they like this new job so much better. Their conversations are much softer and friendlier as is the entire internal atmosphere.

He also told her that the planner parts no longer work as hard as they once did to try to come up with all the excuses and reasons they may need if anyone found out about her. That job requirement was eliminated, and many of those parts are now learning how to write, speak, and tell stories. That is when they are not just sleeping or going out for a walk. They have been trapped inside for so long; they are really learning to enjoy the outdoors.

She started to laugh along with him now and was so happy how everything was changing inside, too.

It has been a few years since I transitioned and completed all my planned surgeries.

I did take a leap into the unknown, and luckily found solid ground to land on. It is not a land that is free from clouds, nor do my troubles just melt away like lemon drops—wouldn't that be nice?

It is a land where I am free to be me, and I have discovered that I can deal with cloudy days and troubles differently than before.

I am not certain when exactly it happened. I just noticed that there seems to have been a weight lifted off of me. When I first transitioned, I was still very much wondering what people would think or say when they saw me. I spent so much energy worrying about the perception of other people, and what they might think. I believe that this was my own preoccupation with a transgender person's wor-

Over the rainbow.

ry about "passing." Do they see a woman? What do I sound like? What if they say something to me? Why do those little kids stare at me so long? OMG, why am I staring right back at them…they are little kids.

What will I do if they say something? There was a lot of worrying going on.

I am not sure if it just stopped one day or phased out over time. I was not even aware it happened. It did not matter who I began a conversation with, strangers in a store or waiting in line for the ladies room (what a strange new experience this became). The worrying about how I would be perceived was gone.

I know that wherever I am now, I am genuinely happy in my own skin, and I believe that it shows. Yes, I own and am proud of my history and my own "I-ness" as a transgender woman. However, on this side of the rainbow, I go out in the world as the woman I am, and sharing my history is a choice that I make, and it is a choice that has no shame attached to it.

This perspective lets me know I am now living on the other side of the rainbow; this place where dreams have come true. On this side of the rainbow, there is not only the space but also the encouragement to keep dreaming.

What I've Learned So Far

Change is constant.

We can deny this or we can choose to ride and surf the waves of life. When we strap ourselves down to a rock, a place, or a perhaps even more important, to a belief, we need to take a deep look inside to assess whether this enhances or blocks our relationships with our own self or others.

All of our cells that we are made of die off and are renewed constantly. Our brains have turned out to be plastic and new brain cells can and do grow throughout our life. We are built to change, to learn, to adapt, and to grow.

Then why is it so hard for so many of us to change our thoughts and beliefs? I am not saying that change in beliefs must reject faith in a higher power. Rather I am saying that each day, each moment, we have the opportunity to take in something new—possibly something wondrous and amazing—and process it in so many ways. We can choose to reject it or to store it away for some future use or to allow it to take us down a new path to explore, even if there is a risk of an unknown destination.

I used to say "NO!" to most new paths offered to me.

I did say "MAYBE" many times, but only to store information away for a long dreamt-about future that I was never sure would come.

It took me a long time to finally say, "YES!" to living my truth, to be the person whom I hid from everyone, including myself. By saying yes, I am now on a journey of exploration into the unknown. I have no idea where the path will lead me.

I have learned to not fear change. To not fear the unknown. I would not be here writing this if I did not choose the path to live my truth.

The Biggest Lie

The truth is rarely pure, and never simple.

—Oscar Wilde

I was very confused when I first came out and started to explore my gender identity. Deep down, I knew that she was deeply hidden away inside of me. I refused to even say the word transsexual, let alone, accept that it was my truth. When asked to identify on the gender spectrum, I automatically said I didn't know (the Defender part at work). I met others who would tell me the same thing, and tell me the stories of either hiding from their wives or many difficult stories of discoveries by their wives.

Each of them shared with me how they assured their spouse that even though they may wear women's clothes and go out dressed as women, they are still the same person inside. Week after week, I listened to the stories. I know I heard only one side, and then imagined what the spouses' stories would be like. I learned how wives must feel betrayed and confused. In general, only a small number of spouses sounded understanding and compassionate. An even smaller number seemed to be willing to continue a relationship with their gender-variant husband.

I heard of their struggles with their partners as they told me of the "deals and promises" they would make to provide limits on their dressing, and time after time how they broke their agreements with their spouse. These men were negotiating with their partners for agreements they either had no intention of keeping or found that the need to dress or express their feminine selves was stronger than their commitments. For many of the partners, they felt forced into a negotiation because they were not prepared for the news in the first place. The shock, lack of information, meant their parts often processed the news with fear and shame. Often it overwhelmed their system. All these situations were problematic.

I am not saying that all people who cross-dress are transsexual and desire to transition. That is not at all true. Many are not certain, and want to explore what is inside them. Even this journey may force a partner on a journey they may not want to take.

They continued to claim they are the same person that married their partner. Yet the only behavior that appeared to be unchanging was that of breaking their word to their spouses, adding betrayal upon betrayal. I heard many of these stories from both acquaintances and friends. When I suggest to them that this continued behavior would doom the marriage, they would not hear of it. "I am the same person," they continued to say and very strongly wanted to believe it.

I learned that this is the biggest lie. For these people, their inner life and their outer life were at war. I know how this feels. I cannot imagine how my journey would have been like had I still been married at the time that I finally had to confront and choose my truth. I had used plenty of lies and denial in my life to protect what was inside.

I am not saying that all people who cross-dress are all transsexual and desire to transition. That is not at all true. Many are not certain, and want to explore what is inside them. Even this journey may force a partner on a journey they may not want to take.

However, no matter what parts of you that may be hidden inside and more so, hidden from a partner, will create a difficult conversation around trust and betrayal and truth. When a couple expects the conversation to be about what is considered normal sexual and gender behaviors, any unexpected deviation can be shattering to the relationship.

> I believe that once a trans person reaches self-acceptance and shares their truth with others, it most likely will force the partner on a journey to explore their own feelings, a journey they perhaps are not ready to take. The best thing we can do is to listen to them.

At First Event 2011, I presented a workshop titled, "If It's Not All About Me, Then Who Is It About? Telling Our Loved Ones We Are Transgender."

The room was filled, as many people thought I was going to give them the tools and scripts so they can successfully share this often-difficult news. I had a different intent. The workshop was really about listening skills. I believe that once a trans person reaches self-acceptance and shares their truth with others, it most likely will force the partner on a journey to explore their own feelings, a journey they perhaps are not ready to take. The best thing we can do is to listen to them. For many trans people this is difficult as they are so excited about their own journey, they may have forgotten that others are on a journey, too.

I have learned that we must listen to not only what is inside us, but also to what is outside of us. For so many years, I did neither.

So far I have learned that I am changing each moment, each and every day. I am not the same person I was yesterday or who I will become tomorrow. I have learned to be excited by this and now look forward to it. My old parts that felt they had to control everything so tightly are relieved because they were fighting against this belief. Change is constant. Change is inevitable.

I have learned that when I tried to control everything and fight change, it took so much energy; I had no time to live and enjoy life. Again, another paradox has surfaced in that the attempt to control things so tightly has the opposite effect and things quickly get out of control.

Today Tessa and I have learned not to worry when our plans go awry. We joke about Plan B. We have been surprised how great plans B, C...Z can be.

I have been thinking how Oprah has a theme that she has given all of us through her television shows and magazine. Oprah shares with us, *What I Know for Sure!* For years I had read and listened and learned from her, her guests, and all the books she has recommended. Looking back on my summer of 2001 as I went through my own crisis, so many of the books and authors have appeared on her shows either before or after that time.

As I learned to open up, I found books with messages that I rejected and denied in the seventies through the nineties but were now easily digested, understood, and assimilated. I was hungry to learn to feel and realized that I needed to be aware of my parts that would immediately say No! and go directly to denial.

This meant to me, that I had to release the parts of me who were always so sure, so certain, that they knew it all and left no room for other thoughts or ideas. I learned that this form of protection was no longer needed. I was hungry to learn how to feel. I was still scared but more open.

What those parts knew for sure was not necessarily providing what was best for me, for the entirety of me. As I have learned to work with and understand the concerns of my parts, and why they were so sure, so certain, that they were the only ones with the correct answers, I have learned something about learning itself. I can be open to learning something new! I can be open to change. Most important, I can be open to question those things that I "know for sure." I have learned that I do make decisions on what I know, but today my most important sense of "knowing" is that I am open to what is new and that what "I know" is really defined by, *what I have learned so far.*

Through my transition I have learned a few major concepts so far. These include:

It is better to be happy and sad...and everything in between...than not to feel at all.

Don't look back, don't look ahead—enjoy the present moment.

Living my truth is an incomparable blessing.

Conversations

Plus ça change, plus c'est la même chose.
The more things change, the more they stay the same.

It was the last day of spring. Almost the longest day of the year. It was a good thing because it was going to be a very busy day with so much to do. Plan A was a day of adventure. I had the bikes on my car and picked up Tessa by 8:00 a.m., and we were driving to Provincetown. We were going to pick up my son Elie and his wife Becca on the way. They had been living on the Cape for the past three years, but their lives of adventure would see them moving in about a month. We were going to bike on the National Seashore path through the dunes, and then grab some food. Following lunch, I was going to get my first tattoo, and afterwards Elie agreed to let me interview him to add some of his experiences of my transition. Yes, it was going to be a busy day, and I was really not sure what to expect.

It was in 2010 when I received a call from Elie, and he asked what I thought if he and Becca were to get tattoos. He was already on the path to living his adventures and truth and told me he was thinking of getting a tattoo of a compass. Being the dad of unconditional support, I told him that if that is what he wanted to do, I would be fine with it. I shared with him that I was thinking of (again) someday, maybe, getting a tattoo. There were a fair amount of parts in me that seemed to be a bit startled as these words left my mouth.

In the early spring of 2014, Elie called and said he was going to get a second tattoo and wanted to know if I was ready to join him and get mine. Finally at this point I really did not need any more encouragement and figured that after all the surgery and changes I have experienced, what would prevent me from doing this? I quickly said yes. Scheduling turned out to be a bit of a problem, and Elie and Becca found a place in Provincetown where they went in early May. I finally made an appointment on the day before the summer solstice and was ready to go.

The day went pretty much according to plan. The biking was a pain in my lungs as I hate the little steep hills on the dunes, and the tattoo took less than an hour. I did grit my teeth while it was being done, but all in all I don't think it even made my top ten list of most painful experiences.

We got back to Elie's house around 6:00 p.m., and I got to interview both him and Becca for about ninety minutes. In the previous chapter, I talked about how trans people force their loved ones to take a journey themselves. I, too, was guilty of never really listening about my kids' journeys, but during this interview, I learned so much about Elie's ongoing journey. I am still digesting all that we discussed. He and Becca are kind enough to share some of the discussion here.

No Easy Way

Grace: I know that you were going on vacation in Spain, and I told you that I wanted to talk to you when you came back and before Mom came to visit you back in Tucson. With my insistence that I needed to talk to you but not telling you why, what were you thinking?

Elie: I remember it being very bizarre and out of place that you had to talk to me and couldn't talk to me. It felt really out of place because we did not have a relationship where you had to say something but could not say something. So one of the first places my mind went to was there was something I needed to know about Mom before she got there, so I thought you were going to tell me something about her being sick or something. It just seemed so out of place that I was considering you would tell me there was something wrong with her by the time I got back.

Grace: So I kind of made you worried. I instilled in you some concern and worry about what might be going on.

Elie: Yeah, you put something in my head. I thought that you didn't want to tell me so I would not worry or be distracted while I was gone. So you hadn't told Simi and Stella by the time you called me?

Grace: No, I hadn't told them before you left for vacation, and I had a plan to meet with them and to meet with Mom.

Elie: If I hadn't gone on vacation, you would have told me when you told them.

Grace: Yes, I would have had you on the phone the same time, because I wanted to tell you guys together and then tell Mom separately.

Elie: So the long version story then is that I spent the entire trip...I am sure that most of the trip was fine and wonderful, but like, before bed or something, I was going, "What the hell is that all about?"

Grace: So there was no good way for me to have set up a time to talk.

Elie: No, it was distracting.

Grace: Sorry.

Elie: No, that's just the way it is. Some things are complex.

Grace: So then when you came back and I called you and probably I just blurted out that I was transgender, I remember you didn't even skip a beat and said to me, "That's great. Be who you are." How do you remember it?

Elie: The way I remember it is you told me you were trans and I thought like, "What I'm feeling right now is, oh, OK, we can deal with that!" I was anticipating what, in my world was negative news, like poor health and illness and like that. The person who I was on the path to becoming...I did a lot of work with gender and sexual identity in college so at that point I feel I was somebody who was kind of comfortable with that topic.

Grace: Even if it was me...your father...

Elie: Yeah, I think you did a pretty good job in setting it up, making me worry about something, somebody else.

Grace: That wasn't my plan...

Elie: Well I think it was kind of a ...shock...and confusing but my first reaction was all right we can work with this.

Grace: So Becca, you must have heard it from him...and were you shocked?

Becca: Well I remember you (to Elie) had to talk to your dad and you were on the phone for a really long time...I was hoping everything was OK and you came in and you told me everything was OK, but my dad just told me he was transgender, and I said "Oh! That's a surprise." That was not what we were expecting from the conversation, because usually

when someone leads up to something like that, it is usually terrible news.

Grace: But for some, many people, that would be terrible
news.

Elie: Right, for many people that would be terrible
news...but what I feel like it is just news...

Becca: Surprising news.

Elie: Just a turn of events... Sexual identity, gender identity, those are just who you are. Like if you called and said you
were gay or are gay, then it would have been like, OK...to me it
didn't have a big...well it did have a big effect on me, but it
doesn't directly change who I am...or change what my relationship with you is.

Elie's Struggle

Grace: Can you say more about what the big effect may
have been?

Elie: Well at first I said, yeah, that's great...and we can
work with that, and we can figure out what it means...but then I
think for a long time, I struggled with what that was really going to mean. And what it was going to mean to my relationship
with Larnie Rabinowitz. There was a lot of time that I was worried about and considering whether you were...dying...and being replaced by a different person or whether you were sort of
killing Larnie. And starting afresh as someone else. I think that a
lot of my worry was that the new person was going to be a
whole new person and be somebody different. You know, that I
wouldn't know or recognize.

Becca: I do remember that something very hard for us
was that there were times you would say that Larnie was like

this and Grace was like this, and I remember Elie having a hard time with that kind of phrasing...wondering if you are two different people, who have you been this whole time. Are you Larnie, are you Grace, are you two completely different people...are you becoming a completely different person, and I remember this being really hard for Elie. If you had made I statements, it would have been easier. I also remember about the first conversation Elie had with you, and what was difficult was that your dad said that he was getting older and thinking that maybe he was going to die and didn't want you to find out that if he was dressed as a woman and that would be how you found out...and you had a really hard time with that statement.

Grace: I think I said that I was going out dressed and that if I ever got in an accident and you found out that way it would be absolutely horrendous for me to do...

Becca: Yeah, that way.

Elie: I don't remember that, but I am sure it is right...

And I think the other thing that is still difficult at times...and it is still hard...I think that I do and Becca does an incredible job in talking about trans and you and everything you have gone through...

Grace: You mean with other people?

Elie: Yeah, and publicly with my students...with all the students, not just randomly, but think it is difficult to talk about when people aren't prepared for it. Pronouns are really complex. I did tell a lot of my friends. I think I wrote an email first. I talked to people pretty soon, but pretty much all my friends were totally supportive...maybe there was one that said, "That was not my cup of tea, but cool." That was the least supportive one. I'm not the kind of person who likes to make people uncomfortable, so talking about trans sometimes might make people uncomfortable, so for example, the other day at the triathlon, I was wearing my Lexington baseball pants, and someone asked me if I was from Lexington, and I said, "No I am not." And could have said my dad is, but then I would have had to explain that my dad, this woman Grace Stevens, lives there. It went through my head so fast, and I just said, "No, I am not."

It's a hard thing to bring up the first time, but once brought up, it is easier to talk about. You know if I get a call...How are you? Great. What's new? Nothing...oh, by the way, my dad's trans, and my friends were all kind of cool, and they know I am an open-minded person.

I Just See My Dad

Grace: Do they ask you how do you feel about it?

Elie: Yeah...with everybody it was different...it was a back and forth kind of thing. I was doing OK. I think I was kind of confused about long-term relationships. I don't think I understood who you were...or were going to be.

Grace: Did that change?

Elie: Yeah.

Grace: So when, how? How do you feel now? Do you see me as two people or one person?

Elie: I think that maybe when we first met Grace...I was thinking that, and it is the same thing now as it was then, when I sit down talking to you...I...don't see Grace really...I just see you...the person who I know. You had all this surgery, and you have all these clothes, and you paint your nails...as my dad...all this, it didn't change to me, you know, your face didn't change drastically enough so I still just recognize you as my dad...so calling you Grace, and sometimes, just stepping away I say, yeah, I guess this is a different person, but to me you don't seem that different in the long run.

Grace: Now one of the things that you have said is that I changed more after divorce than when I changed gender.

Elie: Yeah, I feel the person you were when you lived in the house and up until I was eighteen was pretty reserved, kind of like stiff, traditional, really kind and fun and supportive and helpful but like only a dad. I feel like your identity in the world was Father! And you knew how to play that role like in movies and TV—Man—Father. You did sporty things but you did other things, like you sewed and you cooked. But I feel like...You wore sneakers and jeans and a flannel shirt...and a beard at times...and you were a hard person at work. How's your day? Fine! You coached sports; you just did the traditional things. It wouldn't have been all that surprising if you were the guy who came home and drank a beer, even though you didn't drink. It would have been the classic image. But after the divorce and you went to Insight and other things. I was eighteen and up to that point having the best summer of my life doing my own thing, going to college, and self-involved, and the fact that you left the house was really, really hard, but then I felt within a year you were somebody who had interests and energy...you always talked about energy...and that's when you first talked about Sedona and talked about chakras and energy fields and all the stuff where we said, what the hell happened to this person...you are so different and bizarre...I feel like you made this 180-degree turn and became this person who wanted to talk about things that got you excited—all these touchy feely things...wow this is strange...

And I don't think at that point our relationship was close yet...but I think that *you* had changed. But clearly leaving the house, the marriage changed you...I think that you were so close to being complete as you wanted to be...prior to being Grace. Grace is like the final step in the long project but not that different. Becca and I talk about this a lot, and I hope this is not all that offensive, but I feel that Grace is not as feminine as I expected her to be. You wear a ball cap, and your hair is pretty short. You showed me those glam pictures, and I guess that was what I was expecting you to be all the time. And you still wear T-shirts. You switched all your blue jackets to pink jackets, but they are still like Northface ski jackets...and I think that probably in the long run helps because I expected you to be really over the top.

Becca: Yeah, I think we were expecting a "fancy" lady.

Elie: Yeah, you are not that different than who you were before. You used to wear shorts and a T-shirt and you are still wearing shorts and a T-shirt.

I am so close to the situation, and sometimes I look at you and yeah, you're a lady, but sometimes I wonder how people on the street perceive you. As a man or woman, because when I see you, I just see my dad.

Grace: One thing that I say and try to teach is that when somebody transitions, they force all the people in their life to go through a transition that they weren't planning on going through.

Elie: Right…because you asked how am I doing…now for all my friends who have no relationship with you for the most part, for some reason, I feel mandated to call them up and tell them this is how my dad is doing. No one is too invested in how my dad was doing before, and now I feel like I have this difficult conversation. You know my college friends are important people in my life, but they are not close.

Grace: So why did you talk to them?

Elie: Because… I was upset and they were the people I could talk to. Well, I was pretty close to them…

Grace: Well it sounds like you have a support system, and maybe you don't even have the words to acknowledge that you have this support system…you need to be heard.

Elie: But now it seems to feel that I am holding a secret.

Grace: If you don't talk?

Elie: If I don't say something. You told me it is OK to tell everyone.

Grace: I said I don't believe in family secrets so whoever you need for support feel free to talk to. Don't feel that what I am telling you, that you have to hold on to it. I thought that would be terrible.

Elie: Therefore to me, I have permission to talk about this, so I guess I'll just talk about this, and then get it off of my chest.

Grace: Did it get off your chest?

Elie: Certainly to a degree, yeah, I don't know if it ever will be entirely.

Grace: OK.

Elie: But it is for the most part…it's not something…it is something that in some way is…pretty much accepted now but you still feel like it is not accepted now…like how you were afraid to tell us?

Grace: Does it say something about you? Does it put some sort of mark, because your father is transgender and has transitioned gender…does it mark you?

Elie: I feel we were raised in a manner that led us all to be pretty private about our feelings and our family. The way that I am in my view of the world, ever since I was a little kid, was super positive and wanted to be making people happy. I told everyone I had the best family…everything is awesome. So I have not been someone who shared a lot of my life and my feelings with other people, so it still feels kind of wrong to talk about personal things. I think the people at my work are probably better off because I am willing to talk about it. I think they respect that. They think you're courageous, they think I am courageous. I know it certainly helps the kids because we have students that identify as trans in our school, and I am happy to tell them that I support them. And it is better for the world. As a teacher who gets respect, I can tell them that this is how I feel, but I think it will always feel awkward for me to be like…hey, my dad is a woman!

Grace: Where does that sense of awkwardness come from? Does it mark you?

Elie: Because I feel like it may be awkward for others. Because I don't know if someone is going to get mad or upset. I just know I don't like making people uncomfortable. I want everyone to be happy.

Grace: And you know I am happy, happier than I have ever been, being aligned.

Elie: Yeah, well you have had it so damned peachy in your transition, and somewhere in the back of my head is worrying that it won't end peachy...I am afraid that what if I say, "Dad," to you, and someone gets all upset and they beat you up or something...something like ridiculous that probably won't happen

You Didn't Do Anything Wrong

Elie: I don't understand why I would cut you off. I don't understand any situation where a parent would abandon a kid or a kid would abandon a parent.

Becca: But you started out with a good relationship. If you started with a strained relationship it might have been much harder.

Grace: I feel that for some people, the awkwardness for kids in saying that their parent is transgender may make them feel that their own friends will reject them. That is if they accept

I don't understand how to do anything different but care for you, because you cared for me forever. We all care for each other, and you didn't do anything wrong....

their parents, they will be rejected by their peers, so they have a tough choice to make.

Elie: I feel I may be the luckiest person in the world...you called me... I said that's great...I told Becca, she said that's great. Becca and I are really open, really interested in this...you've got my support, I've got her support, you've got her support.

Becca: We only surround ourselves with people who are caring, open-minded.

Elie: The only messages I am getting and giving are positive messages. I don't understand how to do anything different but care for you, because you cared for me forever. We all care for each other, and you didn't do anything wrong, if you were a murderer or something maybe I'd disown you.

Grace: Yeah, the important thing is that your perception is that I didn't do anything wrong, and therefore, there is nothing I did wrong that reflects on you.

Elie: And I think that is, maybe, how we got raised. Like many people get raised like…homosexuality is wrong…that doesn't make any sense…why would you teach a kid like that? That's what people have learned—so that's what they know.

Becca: Well you were raised in a very progressive town in a progressive state. We are where we came from.

Elie: I don't think it was purposeful that you raised us to accept specific people, more like people are people. We were raised that if people were nice, be nice, if they are not, then don't, that's it…I dunno…

Grace: I don't think we had a home where we talked about any people as negative.

Elie: No, we lived in Lexington, where being Jewish was totally normal and were part of an active Jewish community…and it was never a negative experience…and I never saw myself as a minority, and now I say, sweet, I see myself as a kid of a trans person, so I am a minority again…

Grace: Wow! What a gift I have given you!

Becca: Yes!

Grace: So now you have connections to diversity, eh?

Elie: That's actually a big deal in the world I come from.

Elie: When I did the work in college, when I studied sexuality and gender and trying to talk about it from a man's perspective, it was interesting and important, but I never felt or knew why I was doing it. I think it was just something I thought mattered and made sense to me. Then when you came out as trans, I thought, ahhh…maybe the world prepared me to be the person to support you.

Grace: Synchronicity?

Elie: Yeah. It's cool. It's also wrong, because men have made it difficult for women, and I don't like that…but I don't know why I am the way I am.

Grace: None of us know why we are the way we are.

Illusions

Grace: I have a question here that asks, do you think my transition has cost you any losses? Are there other things beside the awkwardness you mentioned earlier?

Elie: I think because you transitioned when I was already an adult, and you stayed an integral, kind, supportive parent, I don't need a male role model now.

Grace: But as you said, the male role model—I was a very constrained, restricted person.

Elie: Well, there was not a loss here. I was worried that Grace would be so vastly different from Larnie that there would be a loss, but I don't feel that you are that different.

Grace: Interesting, because I feel I am vastly different. Since I no longer am hiding who I truly am, I think I am more open and softer. I think I live in a space of compassion now, to others.

Becca: Elie has said that the masculine/feminine piece has never been an issue for you, (to Elie) but since you always want to remember the good things, and not the bad, the biggest thing you lost was the illusion that your dad was happy for his whole life, before he transitioned. The thing that you thought was that everything was always good, always. What you lost was the illusion that things were always good, always. That was really hard for you: to realize that your dad really did not have a happy life.

Elie: Yeah, We always had the coolest family on the block and always had people over. I had good friends whom you knew who never let me over at their house because they had a weird family situation or a weird home or whatever...and maybe we had a similar situation, but we always had an open door.

What You're Supposed to Do

Elie: It seemed like you were just living your life the way you were supposed to. I see this all the time. Like people are twenty-eight and say, I got a job, I got married, I have kids; that's just what I do. This is just what you do. So many people seem to do that. We really don't want to live like that. That's wrong, that must have sucked.

Becca: (to Elie) That's the biggest thing that happened after we found out your dad was transgender. You said, "I need my life not to be living like that. My dad has apparently been unhappy for sixty years; we need to make sure we don't do that." We always make sure we are living the life we want to live.

Grace: And that's become my mission, when I heard you say this.

Becca: It sounds so terrifying to not live the life you want. It is so sad.

Elie: It is so amazing that you raised us the way you did. You had the strength to not be who you wanted to be and still be supportive to all of us...I still don't get why the hell you didn't just leave.

Grace: It was responsibility. I didn't know people could divorce. I think that the heart that was in me couldn't do that...because I was responsible.

Grace: If someone came to you and said my parent just told me they are trans and is transitioning, and I can't stand it, what would you say?

Elie: I guess I'd ask them what can't they stand.

Grace: It's just wrong!

Elie: Why? I think you need to get to the core of people's value system. I would try to find out why they think it is wrong, and then I would probably ask, "Are they hurting you? Do they want you to be helpful?" The thing you've been good at has always been saying, "I'll support you! Whatever you need or feel." You always say, "I heard you, and I support you, and I'll be there for you." I feel you were always there. I would try to relay the message that if your parent needs your help, what are they doing that is wrong? Why would you need to abandon them? To me, there is no place for negative energy. It might be hard, but in time, it will be better if you just say, hey, good for you. Then they will feel better, and then you will feel better.

Becca: It is hard. If a parent is a good parent, they need to be patient and careful on how this is presented. It is a huge adjustment, and if it comes out of nowhere, it is a big transition…and if people care about each other they need to be considerate in both directions. Just expecting people to immediately be OK and understand and remember appropriate pronouns…that's not necessarily a reasonable expectation. Being patient and saying you understand this is going to be difficult and it will take time and I understand that we all make mistakes.

Elie: We're all dealing with this at different levels in our family. People ask me, "Oh, how's your family?"

"We were altogether for the holidays. Me, my divorced parents, my trans dad."

It doesn't make any sense…everybody's been cool about it.

Grace: Why doesn't it make any sense?

Elie: Because there is supposed to be this horrible drama.

Becca: It is what's expected.

Grace: Here we go. The supposed to! This is exactly the whole point. What are you supposed to do as opposed to your authenticity and what you want to do?

Amazed, I Am!

I was amazed talking to Elie and Becca, and each time I replayed it. It has been three years since I transitioned, and I heard so much that I did not know before. I thought I changed so much, and to Elie's perception, it was minimal. I have become so comfortable with my transition and who I am in the world, I had no idea that this was and could be an ongoing dilemma for my family members. I was right when I said I forced others on a journey, but even I underestimated what that journey might be for them. I hope not to forget that again. On the surface everything looks great, but the depth of thought and concern, and

Elie's comment that he may never get fully over it, touched me deeply. All my parts were so attentive, and many were so surprised at what was shared, in such an open and caring manner.

She wondered how she never was aware of all the confusion she caused her family. She knew that there was a risk of abandonment, and she was willing to take that risk, but this seemed to be different. She didn't mean to hurt anyone and was really glad when Elie said that she didn't do anything wrong. She knew that was true. Still she wondered if she could have made it any easier.

He was listening as he was sorting through all the memories and trying to remember what exactly he was thinking three years ago. There could have been better ways to do this he thought, as he tried to make some mental notes. Another part was interrupting him and saying perhaps not. There was no way of really knowing how anyone would respond, and the news was, as Elie had recognized, complex. Still he wondered if he could have made it any easier.

I chose to live my truth. Somehow, this choice had something to do with my son choosing to live his truth. I could not have planned it or encouraged this if I had tried. It was not an easy path for anyone involved, but perhaps that is the secret of life. It seems that my son and I both have learned to choose the path of love over fear.

My Spirit: Gratitude

Then he answered and spoke to me, saying, "This is the word of
Yahweh to Zerubbabel, saying, 'Not by might, nor by power,
but by my Spirit,' says Yahweh of Armies."

—Zechariah 4:6

Not by my power, but by my spirit. It has taken me a long
time learning this as the guidance for living my life.

Prophet after prophet has tried to teach us that our spirit
and our beliefs can be stronger than any physical force. I can
speak to my resistance to this notion, but it seems that I am not
alone in resisting the spirit within me. How my parts have
fought this. As long as there were parts that wished to hide, being scared, concerned, threatened of exposure, and then shame,
ridicule, and abandonment, there were protectors fighting my
truth from being expressed.

There were so many ways to hide. There were so many
things to hide. There were so many times to hide.

All in the name of safety.

If you really knew me—OMG what then?

What then? Would I be alone? Would I die? My parts operated in fear of these risks and would take over my system to
avoid them at all costs. I was not aware of their mission to protect me, each in their own particular manner. I was unclear that I
could be in charge—I could lead them—and that the risks they
feared and avoided could be handled with calmness, clarity, and
compassion.

It was not easy for me and all my parts to learn this and
also learn to trust each other. In fact, this has turned into an ongoing exercise that includes meeting and building relationships

with parts that may not have shown themselves before, along with checking in on old familiar parts that may have taken on new tasks. Sometimes they still react so quickly and powerfully, they overwhelm my system. Sometimes they take control for just a moment or even can be present for days. Each time a part overwhelms my system, there is a different experience. My parts are like snowflakes, too, with their unique view of what they do and why they do it. Every so often, when I am out somewhere, I get "mis-gendered." Someone will call me "sir." I am not sure how many parts get triggered by this, but my system immediately jumps to high alert. There is a part of me that wants to hide; another that wants to yell at the person who said this; another that is trying to figure out if the person was even paying attention or was trying to hurt my feelings; and yet another who wanted to gently correct the error. Most people recognize that I am so happy "in my own skin" going about the world as the woman I am. However, parts that have been dormant for a few years seem to be ready to renew their old roles fairly quickly, and it takes some energy on my part to sort them all out and lead and comfort them.

I have learned that no matter what they do or how they do it, that they are integral to me, and have my best interests in their hearts. Whether their beliefs are due to their nature or how they have been nurtured, each one is truly working their best and their hardest. I have learned to appreciate each of them and love them all. I have learned that when I can ensure them that they are not alone and that their concerns, fears, and worries can be addressed and dealt with, then we will survive and grow, and we are all better for it.

I am grateful. I am grateful for my life and the incredible journey it has been so far.

No Regrets

I transitioned my gender at the age of sixty-four. Not for one moment do I look back and wish that I had done it earlier. My life has been an adventure I would not trade for anything. There were good times and challenging times. I am continuously in awe how lucky I have been the few times that I thought hope was lost, and somehow, everything always worked out. I have a lovely and growing family and have lost no one due to my transition. Not everyone is so lucky, and I struggle to understand how people can abandon loved ones when they choose to live their truth. My Keeper-of-Memories part has not given up his job or chosen to delete the past. It is all still there and fully accessible—and I hope it stays so. I can chat with my kids and reflect about the times long gone by, and some day hope to share this with my grandchildren and encourage them to find and live their truths.

New Jobs

Back in 2001 when I went through my existential crisis, I noted that one of the books that I read was Debbie Ford's *Spiritual Divorce*. There was one quote that somehow stuck with me, even though I may not have fully understood it at the time. This is quoted from Ford's book:

> In the Sermon on the Mount, Jesus said, "If you bring forth
> what is within you, what is within you will save you. If you do

not bring forth what is within you, what is within you will de-stroy you."

My parts, although providing the protection for me, were holding me back from being! *Being* me, *being* connected, *being* free. Once I was able to not let them run wild, react, and over-whelm me, and create a new kind of relationship with them, I am amazed how important each of them are. On their own, it seemed that they were destroying me. Working in unison and trusting the system, they're all working to save me.

On the journey to living my truth many of my parts have been so glad to take on new and different jobs. There have been so many transitions both inside my system and outside. Some of these include:

- He >> Librarian of memories
- Shame >> Pride
- Fear >> Teacher
- Confusion >> Communicator and storyteller
- The Scientist >> Explorer
- Unconscious >> The kid in the candy shop—feelings
- Arrogant >> Customer service manager
- Controlling >> Accepting and amazed
- Obnoxious >> Thankful
- Know-it-all >> Student
- Clever >> Consultant
- Lonely >> Spiritual

Many of my parts have relaxed and are enjoying their retirement. They are happy that it is quiet and the inner turmoil, the internal cold war, has ended peacefully. They can even laugh at themselves when they share some of their own war stories. They even like the idea of sharing some of them with you as they have been doing here.

Activists

I doubt that I would be where I am today without all the transgender people who have preceded me down the path of living their truth. For many, the journeys were filled with pain, isolation, and suffering. Many people have suffered from violence targeted at them, and this sadly still continues to this day.

To take over sixty years to come to a point of self-acceptance, I know that I did not have the internal strength to be fighting such a visible and public battle that I watched many do. I am in their debt, for what they sacrificed on their path to truth. I honor and have my deepest gratitude for each person who has stood up and been visible in seeking to ensure that we as human beings, who just want to live truly, have the right to do so.

As I transitioned, I knew that my mission was somewhat different. I am on a road to educate people on how we all, not just trans people struggle knowing how to align our inner life with our outer life. I have learned that I could have not told a story like this before I transitioned, and wonder how many people, who will hear it, may think of it as a fantasy. I do not. It was a dream coming true, yes, but it was based on my inner truth, not an imaginary one.

Perhaps my story has helped you to understand my internal struggles and at least one transgender experience in a way you may not have before. Perhaps by introducing you to the concept of parts, you are beginning to understand what goes on in your own inner life, and why you may struggle with many of the truths that you, too, may often hide. In either case, I have thanks and gratitude to you for having the interest to get this far.

I will leave you with two questions to ponder about aligning your own inner and outer lives:

Do you have farther to go?

Are you willing to go there?

My friend, Lori Diamond, has been kind enough to share her song "True" with me to share with you as you think about your own journey. (You can find this at LDFAmusic.com.)

She was saying "yes" when she really meant "no"
And going all the places she didn't want to go and she
Put on her blinders and they thought they'd never find her
again, her again...
And she almost lost herself
Trying to please somebody else
But she won't be a walking contradiction for you
She's gonna be TRUE...
And as he went along with everything that they did
He always felt the pressure, it somehow trickled in and he
Wanted to wake up but he found he couldn't make up his mind,
Where was his mind?
And he almost lost himself
Trying to please somebody else

But he won't be a walking contradiction for you
He's gonna be TRUE, he'll be true...

If you're lucky enough to wake, you'll have a lonely conversa-
tion with your heart
Then you can start believing in your inner truth
And find your way back to YOU...

Now I might not agree with everything that you say
I know that I don't have to, I add value anyway and I
Hope you'll remind me that you'll always want to find me
here...I'm here...
But I almost lost myself
Trying to please somebody else
But I won't be a walking contradiction for you
I'm gonna be true...I'll be true...

"True," Lori Diamond and Fred Abatelli

Haiku: Then and Now

There are places I remember
All my life though some have changed
....
Some are dead and some are living
In my life I've loved them all

— "In My Life," John Lennon and Paul McCartney

I remember learning about the Roman god Janus. The month of January was named in honor of him. Janus was considered to be the god of beginnings and transitions, and was often depicted as having two faces, where he looks to the past and the future. His image was often placed on gates, doors, and other passages.

Each year in January, there are popular articles written about it being the month when there is more depression than in other months, and when even the most depressed day of the year occurs. I do not believe that there is any real research that has proven this, but it started me thinking about the image of Janus. Two faces: one looks to the past and the other to the future. I realized that this image spends no time in the present. What a great way to avoid reality.

I have learned so far to stay present, in the moment of now. I no longer feel stuck in the past or worry about the future. I wrote this haiku to sum it up.

> *I remember then,*
> *and have many dreams of when.*
> *All I have is now.*

In his book *Illusions*, Richard Bach wrote,

> *You can create and honor any past you choose to heal and transform your present.*

I have no need to create a different past, but I do feel the need to own and honor it, and for me not to deny it. Who I was, who I am and who I may become will all be part of my history.

The good and the bad.

The inauthentic and the authentic.

The hiding and the freedom.

I understand that there are people who transition gender and choose to live their lives in their truth and avoid sharing their gender history with others. I fully accept and honor their choice. Again, it is our uniqueness that defines our humanness. As I thought about my own journey, it was clear that this would not work for me. Perhaps this is due to my age, my desire to stop hiding, the belief that I really am not fooling anyone (the grand topic of "passing"), or that just perhaps I can make a difference by sharing my experience.

I no longer really think about endings and beginnings. Perhaps life is really just a series of transitions. Some may seem bigger than others, but don't we go through these all the time? I think we all make these transitions harder than they need to be. I know that I did for a long, long time.

All I have is now. I have learned to enjoy each now as it happens. I am enjoying this moment...and this one...and this one...

LIVING YOUR TRUTH

The Roads Less Traveled

Life is difficult.
This is a great truth, one of the greatest truths. It is a great
truth because once we truly see this truth, we transcend it.

M. Scott Peck, *The Road Less Traveled*

Once we see, once we name, once we claim our own individual truth, we can do something about it. As Peck states, we can transcend it. It makes no difference whether it is the first of Buddhism's four noble truths: life is difficult; or mine—that I am transsexual; or my son Elie's, he wants to live an adventure. We need to learn it, know it, and accept it.

Remember that we are each unique, and our ongoing human struggle between attachment and differentiation leaves us confused as to what our priorities truly are. Finding a balance is the hard work of life as we need and want it all. Can we live in our truth if it causes us to lose those we love? Why would those who love us abandon us if we live our truth? How could we choose?

For me, my internal system is at rest knowing that I am living my truth. There are parts that are sad and lonely and always wonder if life would be different if I was in different relationships. After hiding for over sixty years and battling each and every day, and learning to be open to each day's adventure, I know the choice to go down my true path was correct for me.

I suggest the path of truth is worth considering for you, too. Perhaps the herd will not understand and then may travel on without you. Taking your true road may be difficult. Perhaps someday in the future the herd will understand and see you again, in a new way. Perhaps not.

When you are at the fork and must choose which road to travel on, consider which one you will least regret missing?

Whose Life Is It?

I wish I'd had the courage to live a life true to myself, not the life others expected of me.

—*The Top Five Regrets of the Dying*, Bonnie Ware

In the first section of this book, "The Path of Most Resistance," I asked, how do you relate in the world? Are you a people pleaser, a non-decider, or a non-committer? When you say no, maybe, or yes to others, what is going on with all the relationships inside you? Are your protector parts working feverishly to protect something? Do you even know what that something is?

Our nature—our being human—provides us with the need to be free and unique and also the need to belong and be attached to others. Since our species has survived, it leads me to believe that these are not necessarily in conflict.

How many of us struggle with comparing ourselves to the way we think we are supposed to be or act? Who are the role models or examples that should be emulated? If the model is not aligned with your inner truth, what happens inside you? What is the inner conversation like for you? Are you living a life of meeting other's expectations? If so, at what internal cost?

Whose life are you living?

Whose life is it?

Can you choose to break out of living the life of other's expectations? If so, at what external cost? How do you choose?

I suspect that each of us has our own unique story of how our inner worlds interact and relate to our outer worlds. I would wager that for many, there is a precarious balance between them. How we map, compare, envision our belonging, and the threats to it of loss and abandonment shape us and how people see us. We can battle internally, and no one is the wiser as we learn the safest course is to give others what we believe they want.

First, I learned that I control only one thing in this life. This is what I choose to give to others.

Second, I cannot give away what I do not have.

We learn how to act, perhaps at a cost of being. Or we learn how to reject, to fall into the paradox of isolation. We do this because somehow we have received a message, that by expressing our truth, that is, to be who we truly are, we will not be accepted, and the consequences of such an action will be dire and perhaps not survivable.

I would argue that to not live and express one's truth is also not survivable. We need to live our truth. In addition, it is never, ever too late to do so. I will never counsel that the journey will be easy or simple or without losses. Each of us must make our own choice to take the journey or not.

I have learned two important concepts on my journey so far, that summarize my view of my internal and external relationships.

First, I learned that I control only one thing in this life. This is what I choose to give to others. Second, I cannot give away what I do not have. If I do not have a positive, loving internal relationship with all of my parts, I do not think I can create an externally loving relationship with another person. My internal battles will surely find a way to leak out and become external battles.

Do we know how to be in relationship with our inner parts? Do we have compassion for them and their concerns and fears? Do we love them and therefore love ourselves?

Without this level of internal relationship, how can we have a chance to be successful in relationships outside of ourselves? If it is at all possible, I think it would be rare. If we do not have compassion and love for ourselves, how can we give this away to others?

With the rate of successful marriages being about the same as calling heads at the flip of a coin, I wonder if there is an underlying theme here. How many of us know how to be in relationships both internally and externally? How many can be free to be unique and also able to share and be attached?

I wonder how many relationships between people struggle due to the challenging internal relationships within each of them. Parts will project on others more quickly than go inside to heal. No one wins in these scenarios.

There is another way.

Tipping Our Scales

How do we measure and weigh the possible gains and losses we perceive of living our truth? I have used the image of an apothecary's balance, to look at gains and losses. Living our truth can bring inner peace, freedom from hiding, opportunity for growth. Living our truth can cause losses of friends, family, and jobs. How do we choose? Can we choose the road of love over the road of fear?

For many of us, have we traveled the road of fear for so long we know nothing else? We can get tired and give up. We can give up hope or more. This can take many forms and unfortunately for some they choose the ultimate path of giving up. Some may feel they will lose no matter which path they take. I felt that way for so long.

Perhaps if you are open to work on and rebuild your internal relationships, you may notice a change. Perhaps there will be a glimmer of hope, of a hope that leads to self-compassion and self-love. Once you can see this happening, perhaps you may be more open to choose the path of love over fear and start the journey to live your truth.

I hope you do.

We Are the Journalists of Our Own Life

There is a blue one who can't accept the green one
For living with a fat one trying to be a skinny one
And different strokes for different folks

—"Everyday People," Sly Stone

We continuously ask ourselves:
Who am I?
Why am I here?
What should I do?
Where do I belong?
When will I know and *Live My Truth*?

Our stories continue throughout our lifetimes. We can change and grow. We can learn and teach. It is so much easier to do when we are able to be and express who we truly are, and not feel threatened in any way. We can reinvent ourselves many times over, whenever we want to. When we are able to do this for ourselves, we may then find there is enough to give this power away to encourage others to do the same.

> Have you chosen to stand up and dance to the song in your heart?

Life will have its challenges. They do not go away. Some that are easy to overcome and some that may be on the edge of impossibility. We do not have to add to the challenges ourselves, by spending so much energy in hiding. The energy will be so better used elsewhere.

I wonder what it would be like if we lived in a culture that would say your first task is to find, accept, and live your truth, and then let you know that all the answers to the above questions will flow from that with ease and grace. Wouldn't that be a great place to live?

You, the Hero!

The multitude of men and women choose the less adventurous way of the comparatively unconscious civic and tribal routines. But these seekers, too, are saved—by virtue of the inherited symbolic aids of society, the rites of passage, the grace-yielding sacraments, given to mankind of old by the redeemers and handed down through millenniums. It is only those who know neither an inner call nor an outer doctrine whose plight truly is desperate; that is to say, most of us today, in this labyrinth without and within the heart. Alas, where is the guide, that fond virgin, Ariadne, to supply the simple clue that will give us courage to face the Minotaur, and the means then to find our way to freedom when the monster has been met and slain?

—Joseph Campbell, *The Hero with a Thousand Faces*

It took me decades to find the clues and the courage to slay my monsters. Perhaps by hearing my story you will be inspired to find your clues and courage to slay your unique Minotaur.

Have you chosen?

Have you chosen to hear the inner call, the song that is in your heart?

Have you chosen to stand up and dance to the song in your heart?

Are you willing to meet and slay your monsters, and choose, hear, live, and dance your truth?

Are you ready to be a leader? Be the clear, compassionate leader of all the parts that are in you! All the parts that make you, YOU!

Then, you will be:

The Hero of Your Own Life.

AFTERWORD

My life has been a tapestry of rich and royal hue
An everlasting vision of the ever-changing view

—"Tapestry," Carole King

She has learned to be present, to be seen, and no longer feels that she needs to hide. She smiles all the time now. She knows that the journey has been challenging for such a long time and may yet be again. She is OK with this knowledge and feels ready for whatever may come.

She loves being. She is forever grateful for her entire journey and works hard staying in the moment.

She has a new way that she looks at life. She loves to share it with others:

I awake each morning
With no expectations.

And look forward
To the day's adventures.

She loves watching the snow now. She takes in a very deep breath—and calmly squeezes her eyes into a smile that can focus sharply. She closely watches flake after flake float by and is always so curious to see how each is unique.

She doesn't know how, still loving the mystery of it all, but she knows she is connected in some way to each and every snowflake. She loves the warm feeling that flows when she recognizes the beauty in each one of them.

She steps away from the window and catches her own reflection. Her smile steadily grows as she notices the same warm feeling flowing through her entire body as she recognizes the beauty in herself.

EXTRAS

Deconstructing Sex and Gender

In the section, "The Path of Least Resistance," of *No! Maybe? Yes!* I introduced that the common idea of sex and gender being a simple and aligned binary choice between male and female was not accurate. I suggested that there were five separate and independent constructs that are better used to understand all the complexity that underlies our understanding of sex and gender. The constructs are:

- Sex: biology, anatomy, chromosomes
- Gender Identity: psychological sense of self
- Gender Expression: communication of gender
- Sexual Orientation: identity of erotic response
- Sexual Behaviors: what and with whom sexual acts occur

The widely held belief that has been culturally transmitted—that sex and gender are always aligned and binary is an oversimplification that has challenged so many people in a variety of ways, as they know that their own truth does not fit this pattern. The fear to explore their feelings and to live them has led to hiding and shame when they dream of acceptance and understanding.

I would like to deconstruct them a bit more. My hope is to add to your understanding of the complexity, that will lead you to more acceptance of people who express themselves across these areas of sex and gender.

Before I jump into the details, it is worthwhile to look at and play with some numbers. They may surprise you.

Playing with Numbers

People who are gender variant have learned that what they feel and the idea of expressing these feeling are so outside of the norm, that they may be freaks, and will be isolated and abandoned by their family, their community, and the world.

I have a copy of the *Diagnostic and Statistical Manual of Mental Disorders, Forth Edition Text Revision*, more commonly known as DSM-IV-TR. This printing was from 2005. In it, under the description of "Gender Identity Disorder," it discussed the prevalence of gender variance to be around 1 in 30,000 for males and 1 in 100,000 for females. These numbers which have been widely quoted for decades are now understood to be incorrect most likely by two orders of magnitude—that is by a factor of one hundred!

In addition, the new version of DSM-V has removed the "Disorder" diagnosis of "Gender Identity Disorder" and replaced it with "Gender Dysphoria" (the discussion on this is outside the range of this book). The best estimates on prevalence of gender variance have been published by the National Center for Transgender Equality (NCTE) as comprising approximately 0.3 percent of the population. For the United States, today's common estimate is between 700,000 to 900,000 trans people.

Let's look at this estimate more closely. An estimate of 0.3 percent or 0.003 means that 3 out of every 1000 people in the population would have some form of gender variance. Three out of every thousand can be further broken down again to 1 out of 333. This is 100 times more common than the estimates still referenced less than a decade ago.

I love to ask the question of how many people do you know? How many Facebook friends or LinkedIn contacts do you have? How many transgender people do you know? You may be surprised.

Personally, and without any real data to back it up, I would not be surprised to find the estimate still off by another order of magnitude. We accept estimates of 5 to 10 percent of the population to have same-sex sexual orientation. As more studies continue to understand how the brain is wired during development, perhaps we will discover that the mechanisms for determining one's sexual orientation and gender identity may be of similar distributions. Again, I have no data or facts to support this assertion, but I do feel it in my gut.

Sex

Sex refers to our chromosomes, anatomy, and biology. When a baby is born, the anatomy is the first clue and leads to the first identity pronounced. My own story demonstrated that a huge mistake could be made. The presence of a penis or lack of one generates the announcement of whether the baby is a boy or

a girl. However, we are aware that sometimes there is some am-
biguity of the anatomy.

For many people, the binary definition and debating
points of male and female, revolve around their chromosomes.
The common and universally accepted definition of males will
have XY sex chromosomes and females will have XX chromosomes will often end the discussion. However, once again, reality is more complex. Chromosomes and genes do not always fit
into the binary bucket. Mutations and what are called abnormalities do occur. Let's look at some and their statistics.

Sometimes the combination of the donated sex chromosomes from each parent does not work as expected, and there
can be extra or fewer chromosomes that will have a variety of
development impacts. Here are the most common examples of
chromosomal sex differences:

Genotype	Sex	Syndrome	Prevalence
XX	Female	None	
XO	Female	Turner	1:2500
XXX	Female	Triple X	1:1000
XY	Male/AIS Female	None/AIS	AIS 1:50,000
XXY,XXYY,XXXY	Male	Klinefelter	1:500-1000
XXY	Male	Jacobs	1:2000

There is a syndrome known as Androgen Insensitivity
Syndrome (AIS). People with this will have XY chromosome but
develop with what appears externally as a female body type.
The estimate of this is 1 in 50,000 births.

My purpose here is not to go into the details of what each of these syndromes represent but to point out what I find to be an interesting set of statistics about the different possible chromosomal combinations that are commonly not understood. What is significant is that the prevalence of gender variance appears more common than each of the chromosomal (i.e. sex) abnormalities listed above. So gender variance may not be that unusual or rare after all. Anatomy is one piece of the puzzle, chromosome are another. Our possible choices of chromosomes are far from a choice between only two, binary choices. For those who believe that XX and XY are the only possibilities and that is sufficient to define sex and gender, science now knows better.

Gender Identity

How do we know and sense our own gender? Over the past few decades, we have come to accept that those of us who are attracted to the same sex are wired or born this way. It is not a learned or teachable subject. It is who we are. It is, as I have stated, our truth. We are beginning to understand that gender identity is similar. There is a saying in the trans community: *You do not have a choice in being transgender. You do have a choice as to what you do about it.*

The challenge is to understand that one's gender identity is a psychological sense of who a person is, and is not necessarily based on their anatomy or chromosomes. How this sense develops in the brain is still not understood in detail. However, the empirical data of how trans people will describe their experience and often their suffering bears this out. Children are identifying their sense of gender misalignment at very young ages; how else can we explain their ability to know that, unless their gender identity is based on something other than anatomy or chromosomes?

We are who we are. We are all beginning to learn that acceptance of what is will be better for all of us.

Gender Expression

Our culture also defines what is expected from the different genders: how to dress, how to speak, even social mannerisms. It is interesting how over the past fifty years, with the onset of the women's liberation movement, the cultural acceptance of women wearing pants or even men's clothing is barely noticed. However if a man expresses in a way that may appear feminine or perhaps better labeled as unmanly, they can be ostracized forever. Many have used cross-gender expression to rebel, or to push boundaries.

For people whose inner and outer sense of gender is not aligned, they often look at the risk-reward tradeoffs of their own gender expression. For some, it may start with the clothes, the expression in order to provide some external validation to the inner world. Usually when alignment occurs, the validation will become internalized.

Sexual Orientation

The simplest way to explain sexual orientation is to answer the question: who turns you on? Do you tingle and get hot from one sex or the other, both, or even neither? Our culture says the answer should be dependent on your physical, anatomical, chromosomal sex, and that there is only one correct choice.

Again, the reality does not reflect this. Our response can be dynamic and changeable. Culture may try to instill guilt and shame. Many things in life can impact our libido, and we may be surprised as to who turns us on.

Sexual Behaviors

How many people have been so drunk they woke up in the morning in a strange bed with someone they didn't know and couldn't remember what they had done?

Perhaps this is an extreme example, but the point is sometimes people do things they may not normally do. There can be all sorts of reasons why, and they may be denied or justified. However, people often will do things in a moment that does not fully align with how they see themselves. Sexual behaviors fit into this category. I am not going to create a textbook on sexual behaviors and acts—plenty of those exist—but people can and do explore and take risks sometimes consciously and sometimes unconsciously. What they do, does not necessarily define who they are.

We often use the words sex and gender interchangeably. The meanings and usage of the term sex is challenging to understand as either a noun or a verb. I have tried to clarify some of the usage here in a hope that you can begin to understand the difference between one's personal sense of gender and how they may choose to express it, and all the different meanings of the commonly over-used term sex.

Nonbinary Constructs

Not only can the construct of gender not meet the expected binary norms of male and female, but people can and do see themselves on a continuous spectrum between to two endpoints. For some, they find themselves to be fluid. They may think they have characteristics of both genders and may want to express as both or either at different times.

There are others who now reject the entire notion of gender and have created their own pronouns to be "gender neutral."

Yes, it would be so much simpler if everyone adhered to the simple male or female definition. But it is not true.

Speaking for Parts

As I shared my story, I have not only given you my firsthand account of how I experienced my outer world, but I also have attempted to let you in to my inner world. I allowed my inner parts to speak and share their feelings and their experiences with you.

I am not going to explain the details of the model here but am happy to point you to the following website that is a great starting point:

www.selfleadership.org/outline-of-the-Internal-family-systems-model.html

Parts can and do easily overwhelm a person's system and take over. When they do that and start directing and controlling the action, they are usually in a narrowly focused desire to protect something, but in doing so, do not always see the big picture of what is best for the overall system. It can be said that in those circumstances, we may be talking *from* a part. When the parts are able to express themselves in a system where they respect the self-leadership of the system, they can still speak and be heard, but then we can speak *for* a part. The system is usually in a better place if the latter occurs. A good deal of the therapeutic work that can be accomplished is learning how to speak for your parts rather than from them.

I hope that giving voice to both "She" and "He," along with my own voice of "I" in this book, has provided you a sense of the model's framework and how useful it can be to understand why we do the things we do.

At first, it was challenging for me to go in and find the parts and see if they could go back and share what was going on for them. It became easier as we all progressed together. There is a funny part that has watched the entire writing experience and let me know that he thinks I am making this all up. I listen to him, too, and let him know that he is entitled to his opinion. For me, it felt real. In fact, some of it felt very difficult to take in and understand what they lived through. So many of those feelings were blocked out by all the times I referred to as being unconscious. That protector part was a busy one.

Writing this was an amazing and interesting experience that I felt compelled to do. I hope that you and many of your parts have enjoyed it, and hopefully, learned from it as much as I and mine have.

The Backstory: Coming Out Letters

From 2009 through 2011, I wrote three different coming out letters. The first was to my neighbors, who would be seeing me coming and going. I had no close relationships with any of them. I remember slipping copies under their doors on Memorial Day weekend in 2009. Few gave feedback until I had the nerve to ask if they had received them. No one had any issue.

Another was to my kids and ex-wife. I ended up talking first and then leaving the letter with them. The feedback I received about the details in the letters was minimal. This was also done in the spring of 2009.

In 2011, I wrote a long letter for my co-workers and managers that was given out at the training sessions a week before I returned to work. The details in this letter did lead to many interesting conversations. I have already shared these letters with many people as they pursue their journeys.

These letters tell much of my story in a straightforward manner. I hope that as you read them, you can see much more of my inner story and the concerns my parts went through before I reached the self-acceptance and decision to transition. The backstory and the hidden story that you now know represent the huge mass of the hidden iceberg of what I lived through. I suspect most of us have as much hidden under the surface of our lives as that others see. You may find it interesting to look at these and compare them to the story you have just read.

As I finish, let me share my deepest gratitude to you for letting me share my story with you. Please remember that all your parts are always welcomed, and at each crossroad you encounter, please consider choosing love over fear.

Enjoy your journey

—Grace

Letter to My Neighbors

May 24, 2009

Hello Neighbors. I guess it is somewhat unusual to receive a note like this. First, I would like to wish you all a happy Memorial Day weekend. I am sending this note to you all because I would like to share with you some of the changes that have been occurring in my life over the past few years.

Some of you may know that I have been working in the high-tech field, in a variety of engineering and management positions, for the past forty years. In addition to this, for the past 4 years I have returned to school and this past Saturday, May 16, 2009, I graduated from Lesley University with a Master's Degree in Counseling Psychology. I am now trained as a mental health counselor. For the past year I have interned at a substance abuse clinic where I have facilitated substance abuse groups for both men and women; taught alcohol and drug education classes for teens and adults; provided counseling for both individuals and families; and performed alcohol and drug evaluations for people from ages 13-60. As you can imagine this is a very different skill set than designing computers and managing technical development projects.

Now that I have graduated, I will be continuing to work in the tech field full time, and I am also working part time at the substance abuse clinic. In addition, I expect that I will soon be seeing clients as I build my own practice. At this time, as I start out, I may have clients come to my apartment. Part of this note is to let you know that this may occur.

As I learned during my training, counselors or therapists do not really "fix" anyone. The best they can do is to be a "wise fellow traveler" along another person's journey. As such, the practice that I am creating will be called, "Fellow Traveler Counseling and Coaching."

Although I have recent experience with substance abuse, the focus of the work I am planning on doing will be around issues of identity formation and its impact on individual's lives. Developmental theory indicates that when people struggle with their own identity it becomes difficult for them to have successful intimate relationships with others. To me, it seems that a good deal of the difficulty in relationships and the in-

credibly high divorce rate today is due to the underlying issue of individuals not really having a good sense of their
own individual identity.

Identity issues can be around sexual orientation, gender
identity confusion, codependent relationships between children and parents where boundaries are so muddled that en-
gulfment and enmeshment rule—people do not know where
they start and end! Each of these issues are difficult for an
individual to at first recognize and then to actually face and
try to deal with.

The reason that this area is interesting to me is that I myself
have struggled with my own identity issues for my entire life.
I have now come to terms with my own struggle with the issue of gender identity. At this time I can admit that I identify
as being transgender. Clinically this is referred to as Gender
Identity Disorder or Gender Dysphoria. More and more research is beginning to show that this is not really a disorder
but a natural variant of human behavior and most probably
has a biological basis for occurring. Statistics are showing
that gender identity issues impact as much as 1 percent of
the population. This means that for every 100 people you
may know, there is a good chance that 1 person may have
an underlying issue with their gender identity. This compares
to the statistics around sexual orientation where about 10
percent of the population is oriented to same sex-
relationships. Another fact is that sexual orientation and gender identity are totally independent of each other.

As I have become more comfortable in my own identity, I
have become more comfortable in expressing this by going
out as a female. To date, I am not sure if anyone has seen
me come or go and wonder what is going on or who that
person is. Part of my sharing this with each of you is to be
proactive and let you know that you may see me come and

go expressing this part of myself. My own therapist has indicated that research has shown that it is better to be proactive such as this. I am also aware that for some of you, there are children involved and that it is better to have some information about this than be surprised.

I expect that upon reading this each of you may have a variety of feelings. You may be surprised, confused, shocked, or even angry. You may be understanding or compassionate. Many of you have seen me and my friend come and go or meet to go biking. We have been friends for six years and she has known about this part of me for the entire time. Her first response was "whatever floats your boat!" You are probably aware how many businesses and states are beginning to add equal rights protection to cover issues of gender identity. Most likely, within a few years this issue will be much more understood and not that big of a deal. We see children coming out and transitioning earlier and earlier in life with understanding parents. What is important to understand is that it is a normal variant of being human.

I am happy and more than willing to chat with each of you about any of this if you desire. I hope that after you read and digest this you will reach the point of understanding and compassion, but I fully understand that this may not be so. Also, as I am now attempting to create a practice, if there is anyone that you may know who struggles with any of the issues I discussed, perhaps I can be of service to them.

I am sorry if anything I have shared will cause you any distress. The entire issue of identity and feeling comfortable to be one's true self is so fraught with the fear of how other people will respond keeps people isolated and living in their personal "closets" for a long time. Part of the work I hope to do, is to help people feel better about themselves, so they can better relate with others. —Larnie

Letter to My Family

My Recent Journey

Over the past four years, I have been going to Lesley University, and it seems quite unbelievable that if all goes well, on May 16, 2009, I will graduate with a Master's Degree in Counseling Psychology, with a specialization in Professional Counseling. Who would have thought such a thing would be possible? As you have all grown up with me, I would hazard a guess that you are each surprised that I would pursue such a course. Another guess that I make is that a good part of the reason I and my classmates pursue such a course is not only to help others but perhaps even more so, to find a way to deal with their own personal issues and demons. For me, I have been wrestling with my own "demons" for most of my life. I cannot say that I have wrestled them to the ground, but as it turns out my journey has now led me to the point where I am coming to terms with them. I have fought this battle alone for most of my life. I am now at a point where I am now in a place where I no longer need to do this.

I hope that by sharing this story—my journey—with you, you will be able to understand some of the struggles I have gone through. I hope that you can read this with compassion and understanding, and above all accept that this is my journey of discovery. One that I have buried deeply and am now finding a way to accept and deal with.

By now, you must be saying to yourself, Oh, my god! What is going on here? How bad can this be? Well, now I don't think it is really all that bad, but it sure has taken me some time to get here.

If I were to be diagnosed, it would be called GID, Gender Identity Disorder. You probably have heard this through the media as being Transgender. I have struggled ever since I was a child of about 8 or 9 wondering what was wrong with me as I really was struggling with my identity as a little boy. I never, repeat never, shared this with anyone while I grew up. I certainly found ways to survive and compensate and perhaps overcompensate for these feelings. As a child I would try on my mother's clothes when she was not home. When I lived on my own, I had women's clothes that I would wear in my apartment. I never went outside as I was so afraid, so ashamed, and so guilty for my feelings. (It turns out that this is a pretty common story.) Before the internet, there was little if any information available about this, and I certainly felt like I was alone and a freak. On top of this I was sexually oriented and attracted to girls, so you can imagine how confused I was. So my life was one of hiding, shame, guilt, and compensation. There is so much more detail about this that I would be willing to share if any of you desire.

OK, so there is the big secret! Are you still there? I wonder what you are feeling as you have read this. It may be shock, it may be dismay, it may be compassion. Once again, I will repeat this is not about you guys; it is about me and who I really am. In a recent book by Jenny Boylan, who is a transsexual woman, who is a professor of English at Colby, she said that living under a mountain of lies and secrets has made her ungrounded. I can understand those feelings. I am tired of hiding from you, my family. You probably know that I never had any friends, close or otherwise. I was never able to take the risk of getting close to people as I was in fear they would find my "secret." Unfortunately this was also true in my marriage. XXXXXXX, I do not blame you if your response is one of anger. I probably would respond in the same way. I was never at a point where I felt safe, secure, and willing to open myself up to discuss this underlying part of me. For what it may be worth I am sorry for this. I do not think there would have been anything that you could have said or done at that time as I was not anywhere near ready to deal with it. Again, this is about me, not about any of you.

How did my journey get to the point where I am now sharing this with you? As you know after Mom and I split up, I started going to Insight. Elie has actually seen a little bit of it in action. Well in October of 2002, I met a young woman who was at a few of the same seminars I was at. We started to hang out together as we both found that we were able to talk about ourselves and our "issues." It appeared that this was going to be a close relationship, and I was so scared to get into any relationship with my underlying secret. On Valentine's Day in 2003, I sort of had a bit of a breakdown and told her that I was a cross-dresser. I was ready to have this relationship be over, and I would not have been able to start another relationship and hide my underlying truth (whatever it was at the time). To my shock, and joy, her response was, "whatever floats your boat! I like who you are, whatever you do!" Our relationship is interesting as for both of us, we are the best friend that each of us never had, and have learned that it is safe to share our innermost feelings without judgment or criticism. We continue to be each other's best friend as we both try to figure out how we are growing as individuals and relating to the rest of the world. This was step 1 in my journey. My secret was shared with one other person. She never took part in it, but was always supportive of me in understanding it was part of who I am. In fact, it was my friend who has named my female persona.

Now let me talk about my journey at Lesley. I certainly went to Lesley under the impression that I wanted to work on relationship issues with couples and families. I was still having a fair amount of denial and unwilling to face my own transgender nature. Last Spring I enrolled in a class called

Counseling Lesbians, Gay, Bisexual and Transgender. When I saw the class, I knew that I had to find a way to deal with my own self. From the day I signed up for this class, I had extreme anxiety around this being the first place I would "come out" as being transgender.

Well, it was last March and April that this occurred, and I did a presentation on counseling transgender clients and as part of that I did come out to the class. Once I was in front of the room talking and teaching and showing pictures of myself I was fine. The class was compassionate and understanding. I figured if I couldn't come out in a counseling class at Lesley, where the hell could I do this? What I was beginning to understand was that there would be no way I could in good faith, even attempt to counsel others until I came to terms with my own demons, and my own issues. I was tired of being alone and feeling alone and trapped with these feelings. In May 2008, I took another giant step, not without a great deal of anxiety. There is a support group for transgender folks in Waltham called The Tiffany Club. It took me many weeks to get the courage to call and then to actually go, but this has changed my life. Tiffany Club advertises on their website that "You Are not Alone." This has turned out to be very true. I won't belabor the point, but I have found a place where there are others like me, and I can say that I now have friends in my life. We all are different levels of struggle. Some people are hidden to their families; some are out to them. But we are able to talk and discuss these issues. At The Tiffany Club there are cross-dressers and transsexual women and men. It is open to all people who are gender variant.

Tiffany Club had its annual convention from Jan 14-18 at the Marriot in Peabody. I was there for 4 days going to workshops and enjoying the atmosphere of around 500 folks from all over the country who fit under the transgender umbrella. I have found community and friends.

Where is my journey going? I bet you are wondering. This is a good question, and I have been wondering a lot about it myself. I am trying to come to terms with whom I really am and where I want to go. Sure it may sound crazy, but it really isn't. I have seen research papers that say the prevalence of transgender feeling in the adult male population can be as large as 1 in 100. That would mean for every 100 people you know 1 would be transgender. This compares to the homosexual prevalence of about 1 in 10. As for transsexuals, the numbers look to be somewhere between 1 in 1500 to 1 in 2000. These are much better odds than winning the lottery. At this point in my life, I no longer want to hide. I want to be open and honest with you, my family. The fear of sharing this is that you are shocked and want no part of me. I hope this is not the case. I have reached the point of self-acceptance and let go of the fear, the guilt, and the shame. I hope that I may even be able to do counseling for people like me too.

Here are a few facts. Gender is not binary. Sexual orientation and gender identity are completely separate issues. I have come to peace with who I am. I have found friends and community that I have never been willing to have before. I am on a new journey and have no idea where it will lead me. I hope that you will be understanding and compassionate to me. I am willing to talk to each of you either individually or together (I can set up a conference call) and answer any and all questions you may have. I will not force any of what I do on you. I am not planning transitioning now, or any time soon. However, I am increasingly going out in a female role, and am finding this easier to do. I find that most people just ignore me. You have my permission to share this with anyone who you think can help you sort through your own feelings about this. (As I said I am so tired of hiding.)

There is now a good deal of positive information on the issue of being transgender available if you want to pursue it. The keynote speaker last week is the woman who recently won a lawsuit against the library of congress which offered her a job when they thought she was a woman, but rescinded the offer when they found out she was a transsexual woman. She said being transgender is not a sin against man or god. No one asked to be transgender, just as no one asks to be black or gay or short. It is just who you are. The trick is how best to deal with it.

Simi, Stella, and Elie, no matter what happens I am and will always be your dad, and I love you guys with all my heart. I am now finding a way to love myself the same way.

Love to all,

Dad

Letter to My Co-Workers

What's happening with Larnie?

For most of you, when you read this letter, I will be out on medical leave. Let me explain why. Just like in the cartoon here [Note: Gary Larson cartoon with elephant hiding behind couple's dresser], I have realized that the "elephant" in me cannot hide forever. My "elephant" is the struggle that I have had for most of my life that has been formally diagnosed as Gender Identity Disorder (GID), or more commonly referred to as transsexualism. What this means is that for people like me, how we feel inside ourselves—in terms of the gender of who we believe we are, is in conflict with their biological sex. For most people, the concept of sex and gender are indistinguishable. So if you are a bit confused by what I am saying here, can you try to imagine how it has been for me in first trying to understand it and now coming to terms and accepting it? GID is the preferred clinical term of the condition that I have, and it really has very little to do with sex, but in needing a noun to describe a person with this condition, I will use the term transsexual for someone who has GID.

As I said, most people really never think about any differences between gender and sex. The truth is that there are some major differences between sex, gender, and sexual orientation. In fact, even within some of these, there are differences in how one may feel or identify themselves with how they will show or express themselves. I'll try a short explanation here:

Biological Sex: What our anatomy, chromosomes, and hormones define as male or female.

Gender Identity: This is commonly a psychological sense of self. It is how we internally feel—either male or female.

Gender Expression: This is how we communicate gender. A very social construct that can include clothes, speech, mannerisms.

Sexual Orientation: This is who we are attracted to; our identity of erotic response—are we turned on my males or females?

What may be simple for most people, sometimes can be very complex and confusing for others.

Although there are many theories of why some people have this condition, it is becoming more understood and accepted in the medical and psychological communities that people who have this condition really have no choice about it—it is just how they are "wired" from birth. However, they do have a choice of what they do about it, and for many of us, me included, this has been a struggle for many decades.

My struggle has included dealing with shame, fear, confusion, anger, and potential loss. For me, I have reached a point where I have come to terms with many of these issues and realize I can no longer hide who I truly am.

In November of 2009, I recognized that I am strong enough to transition from living and expressing myself in the male role that I have lived all my life to the female role that represents how I have always experienced as my authentic self. Some of you may have seen changes in me over the past year. I have been taking hormones for over a year that result in the feminization of my face and body. You have seen me grow my hair out to a fairly long length. The medical leave I am presently on will be performing what is referred to as Facial Feminization Surgery. This is exactly what it says, and by the time you read this I will have been through about 8 hours of a variety of procedures. (By the way, healing from some of the procedures can take 6-12 months). The goal of this surgery is to be seen in the world as a female, without people taking a second glance and wondering what gender I am.

By now, you may be wondering what this may mean to you and the work we may do together. Certainly I wish and hope that the answer is absolutely nothing. However, I am fully aware that each of you will process this individually, based on your own beliefs and knowledge. I know that my action to move forward in my transition, does in effect force each of you to also make a "transition" —at least to understand your own feelings and actions about my changes. You may even find you have feelings not too dissimilar to the ones I described above—fear, shame, confusion, or anger.

I, as the person you have known as Larnie, am just trying to live my very best and authentic life in a way that works for me without feeling I have to hide my truth all the time.

For those of you who work closely with me, you probably have an image of this very aggressive, loud, sometimes arrogant male who pushes, pushes, pushes. There have been a number of studies that show it is not uncommon for male to female transsexuals to exhibit what is termed as a hyper-masculine behavior to "cover-up" their internal feelings. I am sure that this has been a good part of my own socialization. Over the past year, a number of you have commented to me that I appear to be acting in a different, less "confrontational" manner. Perhaps some of the changes I am experiencing can account for this ☺.

Included in **XXX's** employment policy is a clause that states there is no discrimination against employees or candidates based on gender identity or expression. For years, I have wondered what this has meant. I am finding out, and the **XXX** management team has been fantastic in their support of the journey I am now taking. The Human Resources team here in Bedford has been trained on many aspects of this topic in general and my specific journey. They will be happy to listen to any issues or concerns you may have. Once I return, I will be happy to chat and answer any questions any of you may have. Feel free to come by my office.

On the surface, it may appear that I am "just" changing my sex. I hope that this letter helps you understand that it is much more complex than this, and I must go through this process to be an entirely whole, aligned person

I am both excited and nervous. I believe I have the strength to transition both in my life and here at work successfully. In order for me to achieve this, I will need your help, under-standing, and compassion as many of you will be sharing some of this journey with me. Oh, yes! When I return I will also have legally changed my name. So let me introduce myself, I am Grace Anne Stevens.

Concepts and Terms—Not Quite a Glossary

I have used a number of terms above that some of you may not be sure what they really mean. Since I have been wrestling with these issues for most of my life, I sometimes forget that not everyone may understand all the terms and concepts I have used here.

What do transgender and transsexualism mean?

Transgender:

Is a general term for all people who have a conflict or a question about their gender. This includes Transsexuals, cross-dressers, drag queens, gender queer, and anyone who has some gender thoughts or expression outside the binary paradigm.

Transsexuals:

Are individuals who strongly feel that they are, or should be, the opposite (biological) sex. The body they are born with does not match their own mental image of who they are, nor are they comfortable with the gender role that society expects them to be. This incongruence often leads to various levels of emotional distress that could interfere with their day-to-day functioning. There are male-to-female (MTF) and female-to male FTM) transsexuals. Some people recognize this at a very young age and some recognize it much later in their lives.

Cross-dressers (or transvestites):

Are individuals who are generally comfortable with their biological sex but for a variety of reasons choose to wear the clothing of the opposite gender part time. They usually have no desire to change their gender in a full-time living situation.

Questions You Might Have

When most people read a letter like this, and after they pick up their jaws that dropped wide open, they often have many questions. Given that I have been living with this for most of my life, I can say I have a pretty good understanding of it. Let's see if I can answer some of what you may be wondering.

This seems like a sudden rash decision for such a major change. Why are you doing this now? For me this is not sudden or rash. I have been aware of this feeling of incongruence since I was eight years old. I kept this a deep dark secret, not knowing what to do about it, and told no one until about 9 years ago. It has only been over the past 3-4 years that I have not been able to keep this inside me any longer and needed to explore what my authentic truth really is. Over the past 2 years I have been working with my therapist, and my endocrinologist to ensure that my journey is taken under full medical and emotional control with proper support. This journey itself has had some ups and downs, but I have learned to not rush this.

This cartoon speaks to my journey; it is now the time to move forward, after careful thought, and enough time for my family to come to terms with it.

This is so surprising to me. You have been so, so male! Well, I certainly have learned to be socialized as a male—and perhaps a hyper-masculine one at that, and have had a successful career in engineering and engineering management. I have raised 3 kids (who are now adults) and was a pretty good father (if I do say so myself), as they will still bike, ski, and hang out with me. Inside, I was a mess—hiding and shameful and no place to release this. After over a year on estrogen and with my testosterone very, very low, I generally feel much less aggressive and much more trying to get things done in a softer manner. Some of you have seen this and have been wondering what has been happening. I think this is it.

So, you are changing your sex! What are you really doing? Let me give you a sense of the overall process for someone like me, a male to female (MTF) transsexual. First there is an organization named WPATH, The World Professional Association for Transgender Health, that has created the Standards of Care. This provides the recommendations for diagnosing and treating this condition. In order to get hormones prescribed, I needed to be evaluated by a trained gender therapist. This evaluation helps clarify where the client is and what the proper needs are. For me this took almost a year. Hormones were to increase my estrogen level and also lower my testosterone level. My face and body have changed a good deal as a result of this hormone therapy. You have also seen that I have let my hair grow. In addition, I have been using minoxidil to help replace some lost hair and have had some success with this. I suspect that hair transplants are somewhere in my future too. The facial feminization surgery will have many procedures done all at once. I have a number of friends who have done this with pretty amazing results. I will be going to a surgeon in Boston who specializes in this type of work. For those interested, the Standards of Care require that a person transitioning must live successfully for at least one year in their chosen gender before they can get the required letters of recommendation for GRS (gender reassignment surgery). So, I am expecting to go for further surgery—a little over a year from now.

Are you going to wear women's clothes? This is an easy one—of course. Most of the time at work I wear jeans. I suspect that this may continue, but they will certainly be a bit more fashionable (at least I can hope so!). Also, my style is mostly conservative, casual—so please do not worry about an outlandish presentation—and will be evolving; but it will be exclusively women's clothing.

How should I act around you? I hope that you can just be friendly, and perhaps somewhat curious. Please call me Grace instead of Larnie. I realize that this will be very confusing and mistakes will be made. The best thing to do is just correct it and move on. No need to apologize or anything like that. Also I'll keep an open door for anyone to come and ask me anything about anything. (I think asking me about anything is better then you making assumptions or guessing, right? If you find you are having trouble addressing me as she, her, or Grace, the classic advice is: Fake it until you make it. Please try. You can shake your head in private, but I would appreciate the effort in trying. I make this sound easy, but the truth is that both of us will probably have some fear around this.

Who should/can I tell about your transition? Ah! This is an interesting question. There is some standard advice in the community, although I have my own views about it. First here is the standard advice....

Does the person need to know?

Is this person someone you tell everything to, and on whom you rely for insight/support?

Does this person have the right to know?

Will it hurt the person to know?

And keep in mind that

Not everyone wants to know.

You can't un-tell anyone.

Everyone is likely to tell other people.

Now, here are some of my thoughts about this. To date I have been following my own rule that if I share with someone about my being transgender, I clearly tell them that I am not, in addition, putting any burden upon them to keep a secret. I have done this when I told my kids, my ex-wife, my cousins, and in general to everyone I share with. Especially with my family, I do not believe in family secrets. I wish and hope that this will turn out to be no big deal, although the initial news may be surprising and stir up some of your own feelings, use your own best judgment on your own sharing of this. I hope that these letters and the training that will be provided will answer any questions you may have.

Hopefully, I have anticipated some of your questions, and you can see that although this is a serious issue, that I do have a sense of humor about it. Again feel free to come by, even if just to say hello, but especially if you have any questions. I would love to chat.

—Grace

FOR YOUR CONSIDERATION

Questions for both internal and external discussions

- In the foreword, Richard Schwartz introduces the Internal Family System (IFS) concept of Self, which he states, "could be analogous to soul, spirit, or essence." In the IFS model, the characteristics of Self include curiosity, calm, compassion, confidence, courage, clarity, connectedness, and creativity. When a part overwhelms us, it is one or more of these characteristics of Self that will calm the controlling part and allow it to back off. Think about when you've experienced the feeling that a part seemed to take over until one of the calming characteristics above appeared to let it back away. What were your thoughts when that happened?

- As you were reading *No! Maybe? Yes!* were you able to identify which of your own parts appeared and when? To what extent and in what ways did they overwhelm you?

- Grace lived with a secret for close to fifty years before she shared it with Tessa. What is your view of the risk of sharing secrets and how difficult is choosing the path to share?

- What does family mean to you? In *No! Maybe? Yes!* Elie said that Grace did nothing wrong, she was just being who she was. What would a family member have to do, to cause you to abandon or disown them? If you find yourself abandoning a family member, which of your parts are dominating you?

- Have you been at the crossroads of No—Maybe—Yes? Do you have your own process for choosing a path?

- Grace discussed having been unable to balance the construct of Be—Do—Have for much of her life. How do you balance the three aspects? Which elements dominate? Which elements do you block?

- Grace talks about three personality types: the people pleaser, the non-committer, and the non-decider (avoider). Which, if any of these personality types do consistently present and which type do you want to present to the world? Are they the same or different?

- Grace transitioned gender at the age of sixty-four. Do you think it is ever too late to live your truth? If so, whose life are you living?

LIST OF SONGS

The Playlist for *No! Maybe? Yes! Living My Truth*

1. When I'm Sixty-Four—John Lennon & Paul McCartney
2. I am a Rock—Paul Simon
3. Seasons of Love—Jonathan Larson
4. The Wreck of the Edmund Fitzgerald—Gordon Lightfoot
5. Tracks of My Tears—Smokey Robinson
6. Landslide—Stevie Nicks
7. You Can't Always Get What You Want— Mick Jagger & Keith Richards
8. Who Are You?—The Who
9. Hair—James Rado & Gerome Ragni
10. The Last Night of the World—Bruce Cockburn
11. The Impossible Dream—Joe Darion
12. Over the Rainbow—E.Y. Harburg
13. True—Lori Diamond & Fred Abatelli
14. In My Life—John Lennon & Paul McCartney
15. Everyday People—Sly Stone
16. Tapestry—Carole King

ACKNOWLEDGMENTS

I first met *Her* the afternoon of June 29, 2013. I was a participant in an improvisational workshop that I had attended a number of times in the past. I was watching, fascinated by the work of another participant creating a monolog of different stages in his daughter's life. My attention was riveted on the performance of how the daughter experienced being born.

She, apparently, was also watching this performance and suddenly made her presence known to me. There are often times I could say that I have been engaged in one thing and found myself drifting off with other thoughts, but this felt very different. She urgently pleaded with me to share some of her story. I asked the group if I could go next. With no idea what I was going to do, I just let her have control as she shared some of her birthing experience.

In the first chapter of *No! Maybe? Yes!* I shared the story she told that day. I had written about the experience in my blog and kept wondering about her. I hoped there was more she would share but had no way of knowing if she would ever appear again.

It was about six months later in January 2014 when I was in a training workshop for IFS couple's therapy. During a role play where I was playing the husband of a couple, she appeared again, although she was a little older and the circumstances were very different. It was the four-year-old girl who was exiled and never seen. Her appearance at this time was surprising, unexpected, and a lot for me to take in. She refused to go back inside and has stayed present with me since then. By this time, it was almost three years since I transitioned gender but had no idea that she was buried so deeply within me.

By March of 2014, I was thinking of writing a book, but did not have any clarity on how to tie my story with all the topics I wanted to share in a cohesive manner. One day I met my friend Peg Hurley Dawson for lunch, and I read her the blog about the birthing experience. She was adamant about wanting to hear more from *Her*. My immediate response was, No! Peg would not take this as the answer and kept asking me for more, until I relented with a Maybe?

I really am not sure how I wrote this book, as the bulk of the 60,000 words were done in about four weeks as I went deep inside to find so many of my inner voices and then gave them full reign of the keyboard. So much of this book came from my inner parts and the experience of meeting and creating new friendships with them has changed me forever. Perhaps it may be easier to understand that this result is as close as I can imagine to coming from my heart.

My deep and heartfelt thanks to Peg Hurley Dawson for her insistence to hear more and more, for her encouragement and for being my #1 cheerleader. This book would never have been written without her advice and guidance when she pointed out I had missed some important chapters in my life.

There are many other people who have been so helpful and encouraging to me along the way to write this book.

Richard Schwartz said *Yes!* immediately when I asked if he would contribute a foreword. He is an amazing teacher and a more amazing person, and I so appreciate all of his comments. Without Internal Family Systems (IFS) as a model, I could not have told our story.

A huge thank you to my children: Simi, Stella, Elie, and my daughters-in-law Becca and Judy, who have been so supportive of me on my journey and were OK with me sharing some of their experiences and adventures.

To the people who have provided the safe spaces where *She* showed up: to Daena Giardella for the improvisation workshops where *she* first appeared; and to Toni Herbine-Blank for leading the IFS training space where the four-year-old ventured out. And to all the participants in these spaces who provided the safe environment for me and my parts.

To Claudia Gere—the good (book) shepherd, who has taken the random pieces and turned it into reality. There is a part of me that thinks I can do everything myself. There is another part that has finally learned to stand up and say, "Foolish girl, you are in way over your head and need some help!" It has taken me a long time to listen to this part, but I am so glad that I did. I learned from Claudia first in March 2014 by participating in her author webinar, "Rock Your Business with a Book," and then in September asked her if we could have a book released in three months, and received another clear *Yes!* I had no idea how to turn this dream into a reality, and Claudia and her assistant editor, Allison Floyd, have done the heavy lifting for me. A deep thanks for helping me achieve this dream.

To all my early readers for your kind words, encouragement, support, and feedback: Peg Hurley Dawson, Alice Bouvrie, Karma Kitaj, Anita Masterson, Jenny Robinson, Lori Diamond, Donna DeLone, Denise Ventura, Barbara Chlorite-Ventura, and Carol Caravana.

Oh, yes, I cannot forget to thank all of my parts who have felt safe enough to open up and share their story with me and with you. They are listening and watching in every moment. Every day I learn and re-learn one of the basics of the IFS model—*all parts are welcome.*

Grace Stevens
Trainer and Speaker
Endorsements

Having observed Ms. Stevens speak often to various audiences from small group therapy to the corporate level as a consultant and trainer, I have been consistently impressed with her thoughtful, thorough and effective presentations. As an experienced authority in gender education and transitioning issues, Ms. Stevens is masterful at helping people process and connect with challenging issues and move forward. I highly recommend Ms. Stevens services to guide any organization to better understanding of gender differences.

—Rebecca Z. Shafir M.A.CCC,
    Speech Language Pathologist

Larnie came to Genesis in 2008 for his clinical internship as part of his training for his Master's Degree in Mental Health Counseling from Lesley University. During this internship and after, Larnie embarked on a remarkable journey that he shared with us as he transitioned to Grace.

Not only did Grace allow us to share in her journey, but she was also gracious enough to provide the staff with comprehensive training on transgender issues which has helped us all to develop our professional skills and enhance the agency's ability to serve our client population.

Following her internship, Grace has continued with our agency as a facilitator of first offender drunk driving groups (DAE). This is a state mandated program that consists of sixteen sessions of two-hour psycho-educational groups. These groups can be very challenging to facilitate and require a clinician who can engage an audience and think on their feet. Grace has all of these qualities and more.

Her commitment and compassion for her clients are reflected in the uniformly positive comments that we receive from her group members following the conclusion of the program. It is evident that Grace has created a learning environment where group members are treated with respect and dignity, even as they are challenged to identify what may need to change in their life. Grace is a remarkable human being and we feel very fortunate to have her on the Genesis team!

—Lisa A. Robideau, MA, LMHC,LADC1, Executive Director, Genesis Counseling Services, Inc.

With so many students at our school coming forward with their transgender status, we thought it would be important to have an adult who has gone through the transition come and speak with our students. A known leader in the transgender community through her work as co-director of First Event, Grace Stevens readily accepted the invitation to be a guest speaker at the school's GSA meeting. She was gracious and eager to meet our students.

Most striking about Grace's presentation was her authenticity and her ability to enter the natural flow of curiosity and enthusiasm in the room, adjusting her agenda according to the questions and reactions of the students. Grace led with an open heart, courageously sharing intimate details of the process she underwent and the challenges she faced (emotionally, physically, and spiritually) in transitioning from a man to a woman. Allowing her audience to experience her warmth, compassion, tenderness, and her tremendous strength, Grace shared the trials and tribulations of her journey with poise, intelligence, humor and spontaneity. It was truly inspiring to hear her remarkable story of transformation from a sense of *entrapment* to an experience of *freedom*, in order to allow her to embrace her genuine nature. By the end of the meeting, there was a feeling of intimate emotional connection between Grace and her audience, with a deeper appreciation for the human quest to live *authentically*.

I would recommend Grace as an inspirational speaker for any venue where there is an audience that is open to experiencing her graciousness, her beautiful spirit, and her extraordinary story of courage and tenacity

—Anita Masterson, GSA Advisor,
  Wattchusett Regional High School

Grace, thank you very much for your excellent presentations on gender variance to graduate students in our Counseling and Psychology program. You have provided important and necessary information that they needed to learn. Your relaxed, humor-filled interpersonal style put the students at ease. It facilitated open discussion and probing questions which you were not afraid to answer. Your presentation highlighted the difficult emotional and interpersonal challenges that a person faces when transitioning male-to-female or female-to-male. You helped students understand how to support this transition, examine their own fears or biases, and recognize that it is a learning process for everyone involved. Sharing your personal story of transition humanized and normalized the process for the students. Your entire presentation was both skillful and touching.

—Jared Kass, Ph.D. Professor,
  Division of Counseling and Psychology, Lesley University

GRACEFUL CHANGE
FOR ORGANIZATIONS
& INDIVIDUALS

Our fears are like dragons guarding our most
precious treasures."

—Rilke

Accepting Change with Grace

Organizations and individuals will learn how to build new relationships with their inner selves, the parts within that are afraid or resistant to change, to implement change and achieve their goals more efficiently and enthusiastically.

Organizational Change

Grace customizes keynotes, one-day workshops, and motivational talks for groups implementing organizational change that will reduce the downtime for teams while increasing efficiency and productivity more quickly.

Individual Change

Grace personalizes workshops for individuals, encouraging those attending to look deeply within to determine whether they are living their true life. Those who discover they are not will examine why and what they can do about it. Those who are will develop more effective ways to live their truth in both their work and personal lives.

Webinar

Coming soon, for individuals, Life 101: Becoming Authentic, a ten-week webinar, to help individuals answer the question, "Who's life are you leading?"

Grace combines her business, counseling, and personal experience with change to help individuals and organizations learn new tools for achieving desired goals.

For bulk order pricing of *No! Maybe? Yes: Living My Truth*, contact the author directly.

**Visit Grace's Website: www.graceannestevens.com
Follow Grace on Twitter: @graceonboard**

**Grace Anne Stevens
Author • Speaker • Trainer**

ABOUT THE AUTHOR

Grace Anne Stevens believes people can change gracefully once they understand their inner selves, those parts that fear and resist change, even when they know intuitively it is for the best. Through her corporate experiences, personal journey, and professional training, she shares her ongoing growth challenges, as well as the methods and tools she acquired to survive and thrive in the ever-increasing volatility of our personal and professional lives.

Through her speaking and training programs, Graceful Change for Organizations and Individuals, Grace provides training at all levels on organizational and life transitions, living an authentic life, and gender variance.

Grace started her career as an engineer designing computers for missile guidance systems. She first learned about change while adapting to different work environments and roles in the ever changing environment of the technology industry. Grace rose through the ranks from engineer to director and vice president of engineering. She constantly reinvented herself while leading full cross-function teams as a senior level program manager. At the age of fifty-eight, while still working in the tech world, she returned to school in the evenings, and four years later, earned a Master's Degree in Counseling Psychology from Lesley University. She then continued working evenings in a substance abuse clinic.

Grace is a transgender woman who transitioned gender at the age of sixty-four successfully in two vastly different workplaces, the technical and counseling worlds. Grace strongly believes, "We are all so much more than just gender."

Grace is an active leader and board member of The Tiffany Club of New England, a 501(c)(3) charitable organization, which is one of the country's largest transgender support groups. She has been one of the co-leaders of their annual conference, First Event, where she has presented workshops and advised many people on their change journeys. Grace received a 2012 Community Involvement award from EMC Corporation for her work with The Tiffany Club of New England.

Grace Anne Stevens brings a unique combination of experience, knowledge, and skills, along with an openness, curiosity, and desire to encourage people to live their truth.

Made in the USA
Lexington, KY
09 February 2015